SAP Business

SAP Certified Application Associate –

SAP BusinessObjects Access Control 10.0

By

J. Jacobson & Navjot T.

Copyright Notice

All rights reserved. Do not duplicate or redistribute in any form.

SAP AG is unaffiliated with and does not endorse this Book or its contents. All other trademarks are the sole property of their respective owners.

Contents

Before you Start.. 4

Access and Authorization Risks... 5

SAP Business Object Access Control 7

Risk Analysis and Remediation 13

SoD Risk Management Process... 14

Risk Terminator 27

User Data Source 31

Streamlined User Access Management 40

Configuring MSMP Workflows.. 42

Maintain MSMP Workflows 44

Workflow configuration for Change Management... 53

User Access Review 54

User SoD Review... 57

Super User Privilege Management 63

Enterprise Role Management 65

GRC Integration 78

Information Architecture 89

Work Centers 94

Reporting 111

Roles and Authorization.. 114

Key Risk Indicators 117

SAP BusinessObjects Access Control 10.0

Before you Start..

Before you start here are some Key features of the SAP Certified Application Associate - SAP BusinessObjects Access Control 10.0

This certification path will validate your capability as a well-trained consultant prepared to help your client or employer manage and execute key business processes.

- ✓ Associate Certifications are targeting profiles with 1 - 3 years of knowledge and experience. The primary source of knowledge and skills is based on the corresponding training material.

- ✓ The exam is Computer based and you have three Hours to answer 80 Questions.

- ✓ The Questions are (mostly) multiple choice type and there is NO penalty for an incorrect answer.

- ✓ Some of the Questions have more than one correct answer. You must get ALL the options correct for you to be awarded points.

- ✓ For questions with a single answer, the answers will have a button next to them. You will be able to select only one button.

- ✓ For questions with multiple answers, the answers will have a 'tick box' next to them. This allows you to select multiple answers.

- ✓ You are not allowed to use any reference materials during the certification test (no access to online documentation or to any SAP system).

- ✓ The Official Pass percentage is 66%. (This can vary slightly for your exam)

- ✓ In this book, unless otherwise stated, there is only one correct answer.

Access and Authorization Risks

1) Which of the following consequences will occur with the current access and authorization approach?

   Note: There is more than one correct answer to the question

   a. Lack of responsibility
   b. Lack of technical depth to manage user access
   c. Manual overhead of maintaining the access
   d. Lack of effective tools to collaborate with the business owners

Answer: a, b, c, d

Explanation:

The current access and authorization approach leads to the following consequences:

• IT does not own the responsibility for proper segregation of duties. However, they cannot pass the responsibility to the business side, as they lack the collaboration tools and language to effectively collaborate with the business owners.
• Line-of-business managers own the responsibility for segregation of duties (SoD), but they lack the technical depth to manage user access, so they rely on IT.
• Internal auditors are trying desperately to stay on top of the SoD issue. However, with manually maintained spreadsheets listing the access and authorizations of all employees, contractors, partners, and so on, they can only perform a very limited audit at a very high cost.

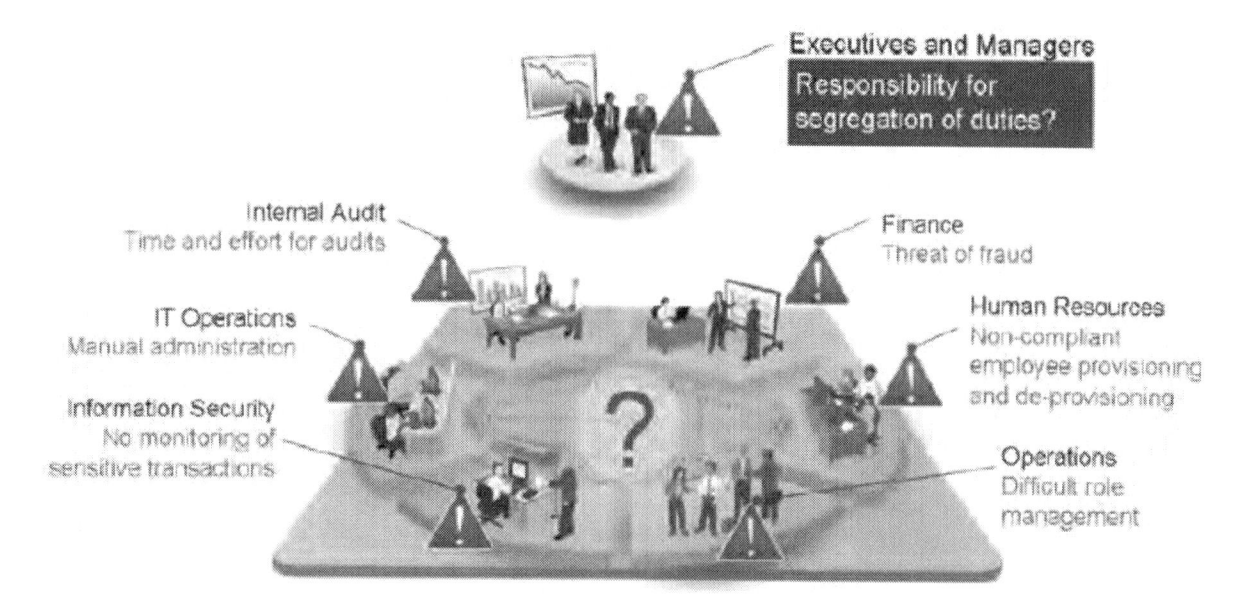

2) Which of the following are the benefits by managing compliance with SAP Business Object Access control?

Note: There is more than one correct answer to the question

a. Continuous audit and record keeping
b. Efficient and compliant user provisioning
c. Sensitive transaction monitoring
d. Improve efficiency by automating core compliance/security risks
e. Difficult role management
f. Time and effort for audits

Answer: a, b, c, d

Explanation:

Implementation of comprehensive risk-based access and authorization management:
• Overcome fragmented authorization management processes
• Effective and efficient cleanup of SoD conflicts and excessive authorizations
• Prevent future violations via a risk-based approval process for new authorizations within the organization
• Business assumes ownership:
Who can access the data in my area?
What kind of authorizations do I want to assign?
Are all risks properly mitigated?
Ensure the mitigation is effective.

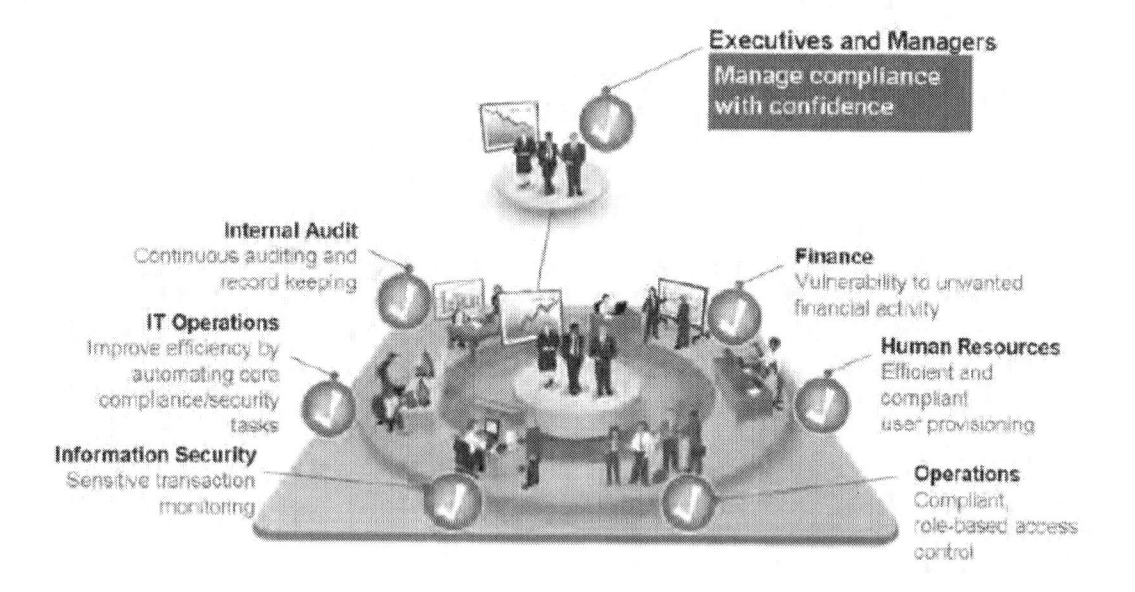

SAP Business Object Access Control

3) Suppose you have configured Business Object Access Control then which of the following components provide an integrated risk based access and authorization management solution?

Note: There is more than one correct answer to the question

a. Risk Analysis and Remediation
b. Compliant User provisioning
c. Super User privilege Management
d. Enterprise Role Management

Answer: a, b, c, d

Explanation:

SAP Business Objects Access Control Suite Components the SAP Business Objects Access Control application is a suite of four components that work together to provide a comprehensive and integrated, risk-based access and authorization management solution.

These components are:
• Risk Analysis and Remediation (RAR)
• Compliant User Provisioning (CUP)

- Super user Privilege Management (SPM)
- Enterprise Role Management (ERM)

The figure below shows a high-level overview of the relationships between the various components.

SAP BusinessObjects Access Control
Solving access control challenges

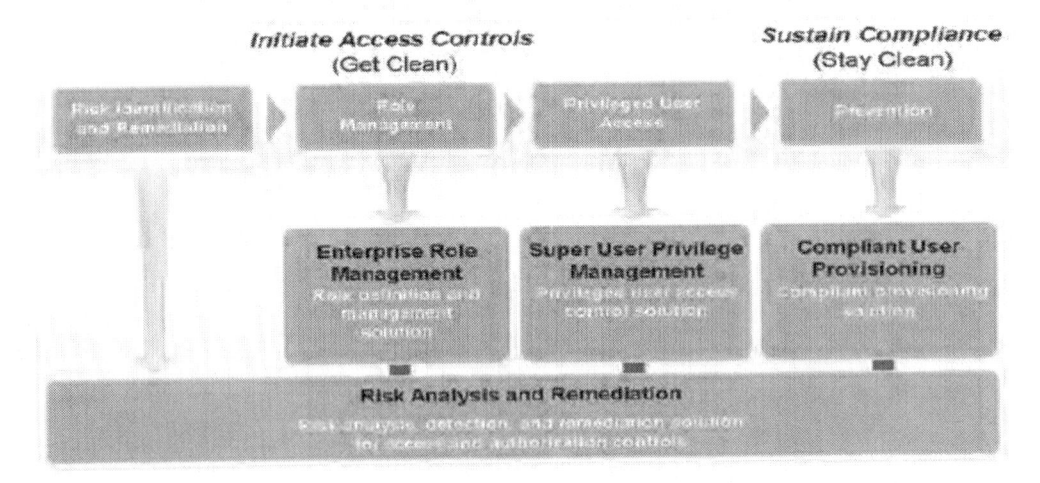

Sustainable prevention of segregation of duties violations

4) Which of the following component is full automated and resolve all SoD and audit issues related to regulatory compliance?

   a. Risk Analysis and Remediation
   b. Compliant User provisioning
   c. Super User privilege Management
   d. Enterprise Role Management

Answer: a

Explanation:

Risk Analysis and Remediation: The Risk Analysis and Remediation (RAR) component is a fully automated security audit and segregation of duties (SoD) analysis tool designed to identify, analyze, and resolve all SoD and audit issues related to regulatory compliance. It includes an expandable starter set of rules. Risks can be identified and created in a system that can be correlated with functions, and each function can be associated with a business process.

Risk Analysis and Remediation produces SoD analytical reports (both summary and detail) for selected users, user groups, roles, and profiles. It also produces reports on critical actions, critical permissions, critical roles, and profiles. Risk Analysis and Remediation provides comprehensive risk management functionality and powerful, easy to use, functionality to document risk mitigation controls. The SoD rule set created in this business scenario is used as the basis for all SoD analysis for the access control components.

Risk Analysis and Remediation
SAP Business Objects GRC solutions: Access control
Real-time compliance stops security and controls violations before they occur

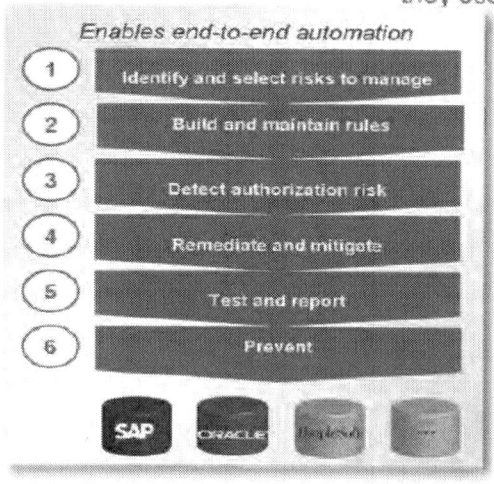

Enables end-to-end automation
1. Identify and select risks to manage
2. Build and maintain rules
3. Detect authorization risk
4. Remediate and mitigate
5. Test and report
6. Prevent

- Significantly reduce the cost of compliance
- Reduce risk with preventive cross-enterprise controls
- Reduce time to compliance through automation
- Be ready to run with most comprehensive rules set

36% cost reduction for managing authorization risk –
Customer survey May 2005

5) Which of the following component is the workflow engine for all of the SAP Business Object Access control components?

   a. Risk Analysis and Remediation
   b. Compliant User provisioning
   c. Super User privilege Management
   d. Enterprise Role Management

Answer: b

Explanation:

Compliant User Provisioning: The Workflow Engine
The Compliant User Provisioning (CUP) component provides a new approach to provisioning that allows administrators of enterprise systems to automate the process, to manage the various types of business risks, and to reduce the workload for IT staff. It is the workflow engine for all of the SAP Business Objects Access Control components.
With its configurable workflow capabilities, Compliant User Provisioning automates and expedites user provisioning throughout an employee's life cycle. By integrating with the Risk Analysis and Remediation

SoD rules, Compliant User Provisioning prevents SoD violations and helps to ensure corporate accountability and compliance with the Sarbanes-Oxley Act and other laws and regulations.

Compliant User Provisioning
SAP BusinessObjects GRC solutions: Access control
Enables compliant end-to-end provisioning
"hire to retire"

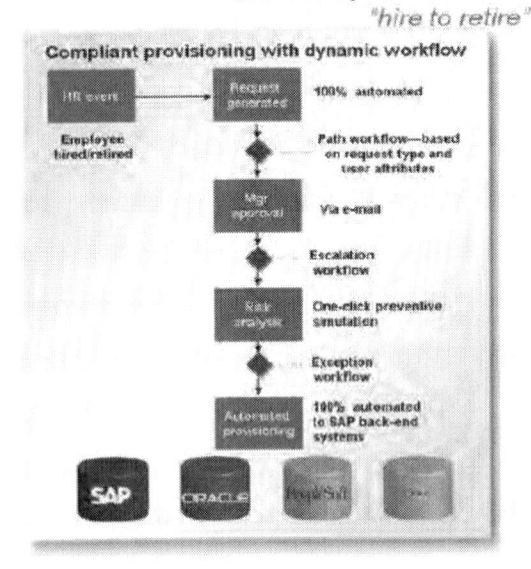

- Embed cross-enterprise preventive compliance in business process
- Reduce cost of user administration
- Improve productivity of end users
- Provide auditable tracking for auditors

"We reduced provisioning from 2 weeks to 2 days"
— Web Seminar Rockwell Collins, March 2006

6) **Which of the following component enables enterprise role definition and maintenance in a single location?**

   a. Risk Analysis and Remediation
   b. Compliant User provisioning
   c. Super User privilege Management
   d. Enterprise Role Management

Answer: d

Explanation:

Enterprise Role Management: Centralizing Role Documentation the Enterprise Role Management (ERM) component automates role definition and management of roles. This capability enables preferred practices to ensure that role definitions, development, testing, and maintenance are consistent across the entire enterprise, resulting in lower ongoing maintenance and painless knowledge transfer. It provides SAP security administrators, role designers, and role owners with a simplified means of documenting and maintaining important role information for better role management.

Enterprise Role Management
SAP BusinessObjects GRC solutions: Access control
Enables enterprise role definition and maintenance in a single location

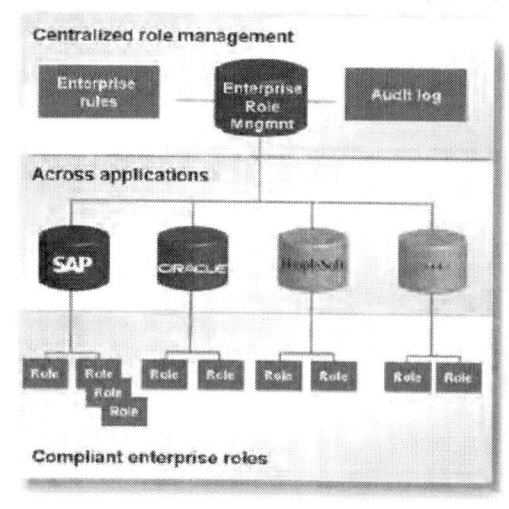

- Reduce cost of role maintenance
- Ease compliance and avoid authorization risk
- Eliminate errors and enforce best practices
- Assure audit-ready traceability and security checks

28% time savings in role management.
– Customer Survey, March 2006

7) Which of the following component enables compliance focused emergency access for SAP?

a. Risk Analysis and Remediation
b. Compliant User provisioning
c. Super User privilege Management
d. Enterprise Role Management

Answer: c

Explanation:

Super user Privilege Management: Monitoring the Firefighter the Super user Privilege Management (SPM) component tracks, monitors, and logs the activities that are performed by a super user with a privileged user ID. In emergencies or extraordinary situations, Super user Privilege Management enables users to perform activities outside their role under super user-like privileges in a controlled, auditable environment.

Super User Privilege Management
SAP BusinessObjects GRC solutions: Access control

Enables compliance-focused emergency access for SAP

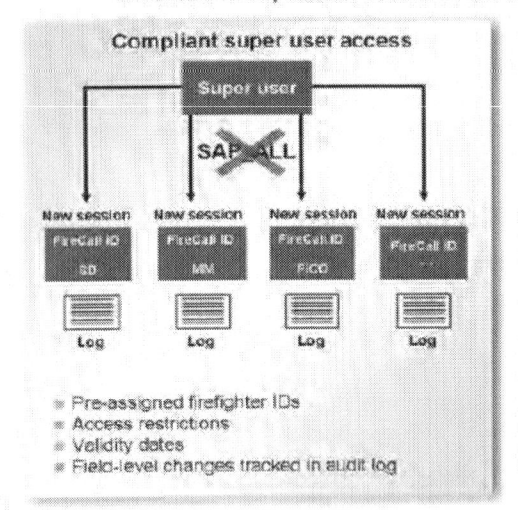

Compliant super user access

- Close #1 open audit issue
- Avoid business obstructions with faster emergency response
- Reduce audit time
- Reduce time to perform critical tasks

- Pre-assigned firefighter IDs
- Access restrictions
- Validity dates
- Field-level changes tracked in audit log

"Super users and auditors love it"
– Web Seminar Lincoln Electric, March 2006

8) Which of the following roles are delivered with SAP Business Object Access control?

   Note: There is more than one correct answer to the question

   a. AEAdmin
   b. VIRSA_CC_Administrator
   c. RE Admin
   d. AE Approver

Answer: a, b, c, d

Explanation:

The concept of roles in the UME is based on actions. Actions are assigned to roles within the UME, and this makes up a role in the UME. The following roles are delivered with SAP Business Objects Access Control:

• Compliant User Provisioning is comprised of three roles: AEAdmin, AESecurity, and AEApprover. All of these roles are made up of different actions.
– Some of the actions delivered with Compliant User Provisioning include: ViewAccessEnforcer, AE.ModifyBackgroundJobsConfiguration, and AE.ModifyChangeLogConfiguration

• Risk Analysis and Remediation is comprised of four roles: VIRSA_CC_Administrator, VIRSA_CC_Report, VIRSA_CC_Security_Admin, and VIRSA_CC_Business_Owner.

– Some of the actions delivered with Risk Analysis and Remediation are com.virsa.cc.CreateRuleSet, com.virsa.cc.ChangeRuleSet, and com.virsa.cc.DeleteRuleSet.

• Enterprise Role Management is comprised of six roles: RE Admin, REBusinessuser, RERoleDesigner, RESecurity, RESuperuser, and REConfigurator.
– Some of the actions delivered with Enterprise Role Management are ViewConfiguration, RE.ViewRoleExpert, and RE.ViewRoleLibrary.

• Super user Privilege Management is made up of one SAP role: FF_Admin. This is the administrator role and should only be used by the administrator.
You can create additional roles by assigning some of the following actions: ViewreportsTab, View Reaffirms, and SOD Report.
All of these roles are standard SAP-delivered roles. If you want to replicate or modify the roles, use a copy so the integrity of the SAP-delivered roles is maintained

Risk Analysis and Remediation

9) Suppose you are implementing Risk Analysis and Remediation, then which of the following items must be configured for the system to work properly?

Note: There is more than one correct answer to the question

a. UME Verification
b. IGS Running or not
c. Job daemon verification
d. SAP Jco activation

Answer: a, b, c, d

Explanation:

When implementing Risk Analysis and Remediation, there are several items that must be configured for the system to work properly. Following is a list of items that must be checked.

Steps to Verify Installation

• Confirm that the Internet Graphics Sever (IGS) is running. Go to http://servername:40080/; this location will tell you if the IGS is running or not. If you see a message that says SAP IGS is running, this confirms it has been configured properly.

• Confirm that the job daemon is running. To verify that it is running, go to *http://servername:port/sap/CCBgStatus.jsp* and to *http://servername:port/sap/CCADStatus.jsp*.
If you experience issues with the job daemon you will need to verify that the lines 105, 106 and 107 are inserted in the table virsa_cc_config.
Use the debugger:
http://servername:50000/webdynpro/dispatcher/sap.com/grc~ccappcomp/CCDebugger for this.

• Verify that the roles have been imported to the UME. It is important to make sure that the roles text file was imported during the installation of Risk Analysis and Remediation. *Do this by going to the User Management Engine (UME)*

• Ensure that the Real Time Agents (RTA) have been installed through transaction code SPAM.

• Ensure that the SAP Java Connectors (JCo) have been activated. Two JCos are required for Risk Analysis and Remediation; one is for metadata and one is for model.
To check them, choose *Webdynpro → Administrator Content → Maintain JCo Connectors*.

Caution: During installation of the RTAs, use transaction SPAM to identify if there are any HR components installed on that system. If there are any HR components, you will need to install the HRRTA. If this is not done, the risk analysis will not complete when you attempt to run it from Risk Analysis and Remediation.

SoD Risk Management Process

10) Which of the following approach is possible to implement the process of SoD Risk Management?

   a. Single Phase Approach
   b. Two Phase approach
   c. Three Phase Approach
   d. Four Phase Approach

Answer: c

Explanation:

Risk Management Phase approach SAP has developed a three-phase approach to risk management. By applying this method, it is possible to implement a process for segregation of duties (SoD) risk management.

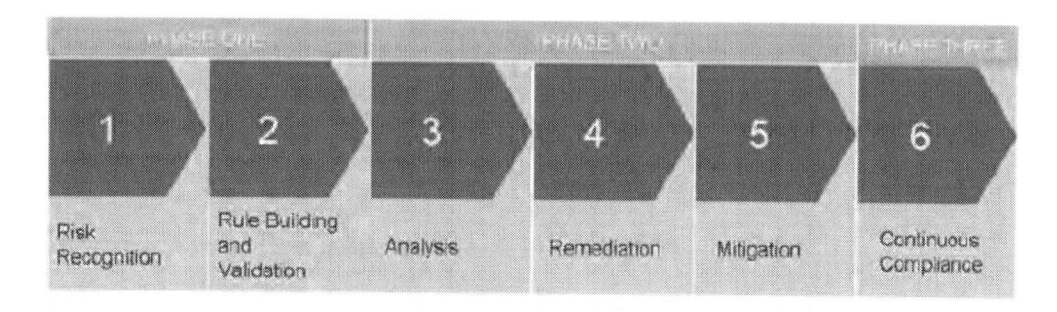

The process begins by defining the risks, rule building, and validation.

Risk Recognition In the risk recognition phase, identify authorization risks and approve exceptions. Clarify and classify risk as high, medium, or low. Identify new risks and conditions for monitoring in the future.
Rule Building and Validation In the rule building and validation process, reference best practices rules for your environment. Validate rules; customize rules, and then test. Verify against test user and role cases.
Analysis During analysis, run analytical reports. Estimate cleanup efforts. Analyze roles and users. Modify rules based on analysis. Set alerts to distinguish executed risks.
Remediation In the remediation process determines alternatives for eliminating risks. Present analysis and select corrective actions. Document approval of corrective actions. Modify or create roles or user assignments.
Mitigation During mitigation, determine alternative controls to mitigate risk. Educate management about conflict approval and monitoring. Document a process to monitor mitigation controls. Implement controls.
Continuous Compliance In continuous compliance, communicate changes in roles and user assignments. Simulate changes to roles and users. Implement alerts to monitor for selected risks and mitigate control testing.

11) Which of the following are the responsibilities of Business Process Owner?

Note: There is more than one correct answer to the question

a. Identifying risks
b. Approve remediation involving user access
c. Design control for mitigation conflicts
d. Perform proactive continuous compliance

Answer: a, b, c, d

Explanation:

Business Process Owner

During the risk management process, you will need to identify process owners in areas such as finance, sales, purchasing, and materials management, depending on where the SoD risks are located. Involving the business process owners from the beginning of the project is important because they will understand the impact of the risks after the rules have been defined.

Responsibilities:

1. Identify risks and/or approve risks for monitoring
2. Approve remediation involving user access
3. Design control for mitigation conflicts
4. Communicate access assignments of role change
5. Perform proactive continuous compliance

12) Suppose as a business process expert you are responsible to build a new rule set from scratch using the standard rule set delivered from SAP as a template, then in which of the following order you will perform a rule building?

1. Create a business process
2. Create functions for the business process
3. Create a risk for the business process
4. Define a rule set ID and description

a. 1,2,3,4
b. 2,3,1,4
c. 1,4,3,2
d. 4,3,2,1

Answer: c

Explanation:

Rule Building and Validation After risk recognition, the second part of phase one is rule building and validation.

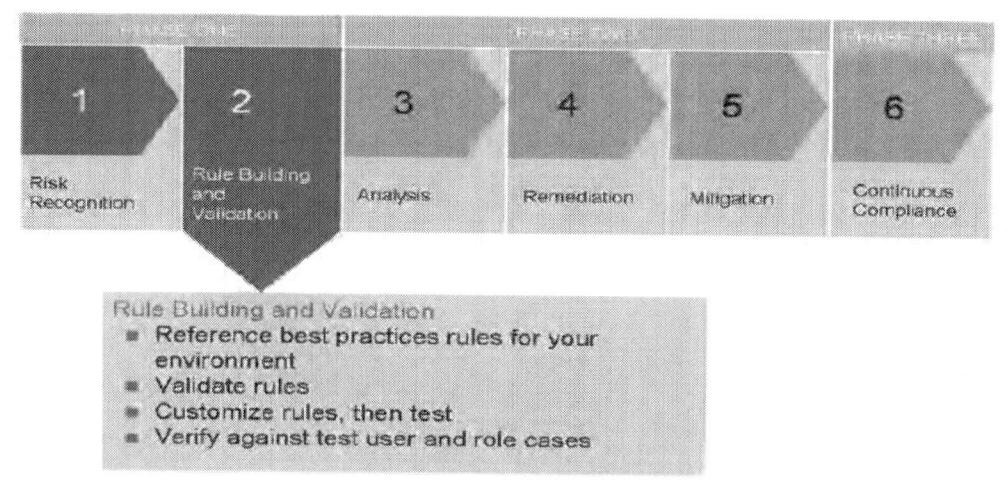

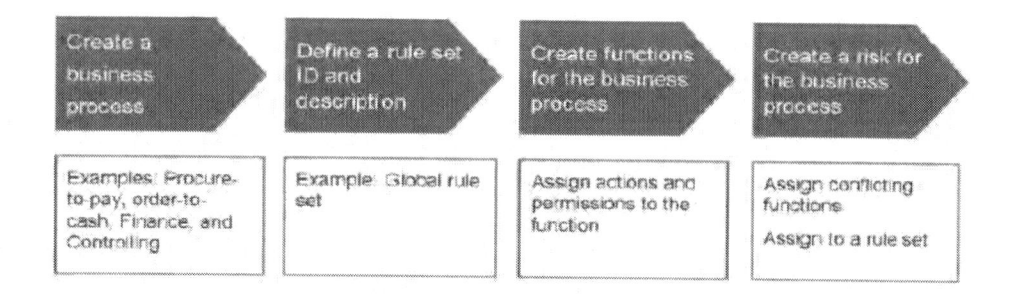

SAP Business Objects Access control automatically generates the rules as permutations of the different actions and permissions derived from the combined functions

13) Which of the following rule sets are delivered by SAP?

    Note: There is more than one correct answer to the question

    a. ERP
    b. EBP
    c. CRM
    d. Consolidation

e. APO

Answer: a, b, c, d, e

Explanation:

Delivered Rule Set from SAP
The SAP delivered rule set provides a list of SoD risks that have been accumulated from best practices, clients, and SAP's own experience you should review these rules to determine if they are applicable to your clients. They are a recommendation only.

The delivered rule set includes rules for:

- ERP
  – Basis
  – Finance
  – HR / Payroll
  – MM / PP / QM
  – Order-to-cash
  – Procure-to-pay
- SRM / EBP
- CRM
- Consolidation
- APO

14) Which of the following option allows to choose the Risk change history?

    a. Rule Architect →Change History→ Functions
    b. Rule Architect → Change History → Risks
    c. Rule Architect → Risks → Change History
    d. Rule Architect → Risk History

Answer: b

Explanation:

Risk Change History To view change log information for risks, choose *Rule Architect → Change History → Risks*. In the displayed *Risks-Change History Results* screen, you select your settings and choose *Execute* to run a search to view the change log results.

The Risks Change History Results log includes:
- Changed On: The date and time
- Changed by: The user ID
- Risk ID
- Change Type: The type is either *Insert* or *Delete*
- Field
- Old Value

- New Value

15) In which of the following ways rule sets can be compared?

   Note: There is more than one correct answer to the question

   a. Comparison of risks in the designated rule sets
   b. Comparison of business process functions with risks
   c. Comparison of risks and actions/permissions
   d. Comparison of actions and business process functions

Answer: a, c

Explanation:

The rule sets can be compared in two ways:
- A comparison of just the risks in the designated rule sets
- A comparison of risks and actions/permissions

To perform a comparison of rule sets, choose *Rule Architect* → *Rule Sets* →*Compare*.

A comparison of risks is **always** performed, and these results are displayed initially. The *Summary* button on the risk comparison screen drills down to an action rule comparison. The Detail button in the action rule comparison drills down to a permission rule comparison.

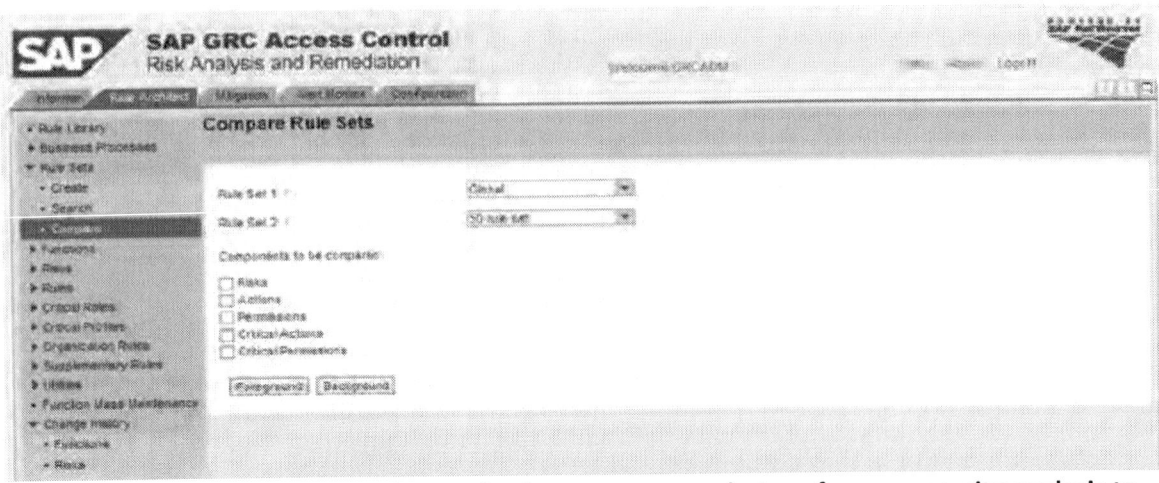

16) In which of the following phase, a business process analyst performs a security analysis to confirm risks for users and roles?

   a. Remediation
   b. Analysis
   c. Risk Recognition
   d. Mitigation

Answer: c

Explanation:

SoD Risk Management Process Phase Two: Analysis The purpose of this phase is to provide business process analysts and business process owners with alternatives for correcting or eliminating risks by:

• Performing a security analysis to confirm risks for:
– Simple roles
– Composite roles
– Users

• Reviewing the role to determine how certain personnel might be restricted from performing undesired activities by checking:
– Objects
– Fields
– Values

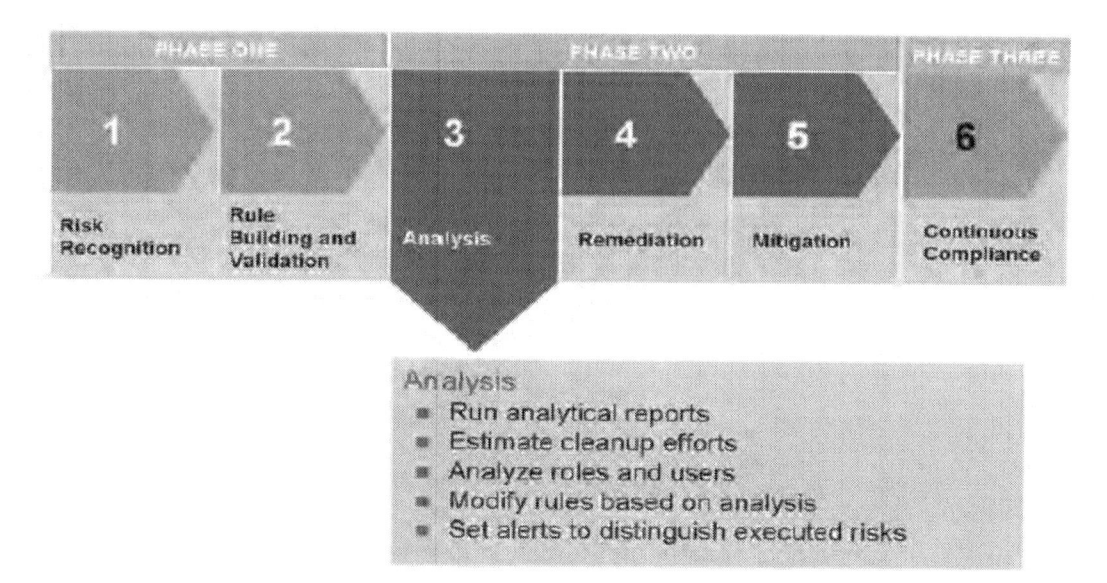

17) In which of the following phase business process analyst will determine alternatives for eliminating issues in roles?

   a. Remediation
   b. Analysis
   c. Risk Recognition
   d. Mitigation

Answer: a

Explanation:

SoD Risk Management Process Phase Two: Risk Remediation
The purpose of the remediation phase is to determine alternatives for eliminating issues in roles. The recommended approach is to resolve issues in the following order:
1. Single roles
   • Simplest place to start
   • Prevents SoD violations from being reintroduced
2. Composite roles
3. Users

A remediation plan should be documented by the security administrators. Business process owners should be involved in its development and approve the plan.

Phase Two: Remediation

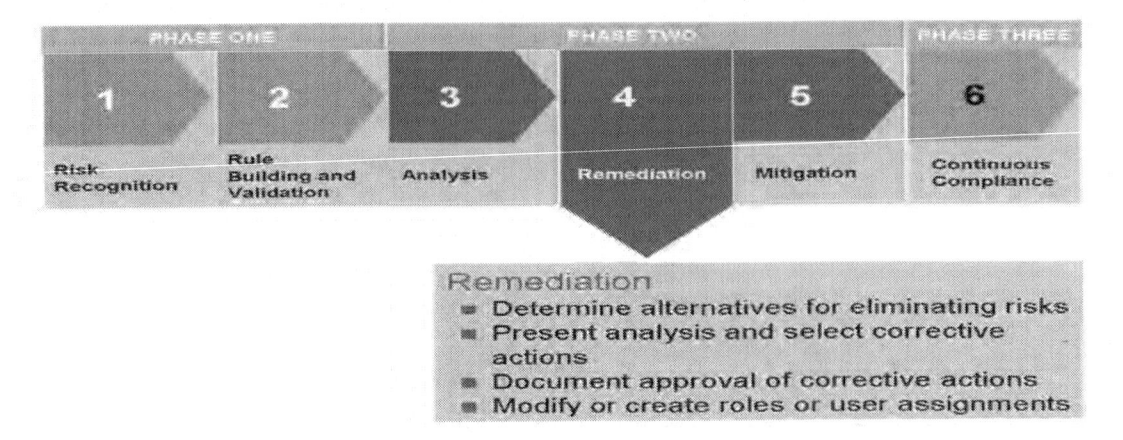

Remediation
- Determine alternatives for eliminating risks
- Present analysis and select corrective actions
- Document approval of corrective actions
- Modify or create roles or user assignments

18) In which of the following cases Simulation takes place in Risk Analysis screen?

    Note: There is more than one correct answer to the question

    a. Add or remove an action
    b. Decide whether to add or remove a value
    c. Specify value for simulation
    d. Add or remove a role

Answer: a, b, c, d

Explanation:

Simulation
Simulation takes place in the *Risk Analysis* screen:
- Decide whether to add or remove a value:
    - To add, choose Exclude = No.
    - To remove, choose Exclude = Yes.
- Decide which objects should be included in the simulation:
    - Add or remove an action.
    - Add or remove a role.
    - Add or remove a profile.
- Specify the values for simulation.

19) Which of the following statements may lead to resolution of SoD Violation?

    Note: There is more than one correct answer to the question

    a. SoD violation caused by an incorrect rule
    b. SoD violation can be addressed using alternatives SAP Workflow, user exits
    c. Checking Super user privilege management possibility
    d. Access removal from user checking

Answer: a, b, c, d

Explanation:

Remediation
Remediation means correcting or eliminating SoD violations.
1. Is this SOD violation caused by an incorrect rule? If so, modify rule to resolve false positive.
2. Can access be removed from the role or user?
3. Address SoD violation by using alternatives:
   - SAP workflow
   - User exits
   - Configuration modifications
   - Business process change
4. Check if super user privilege management is possible.

Note: If the SoD violation is not resolved in steps 1 to 4, mitigation is required.

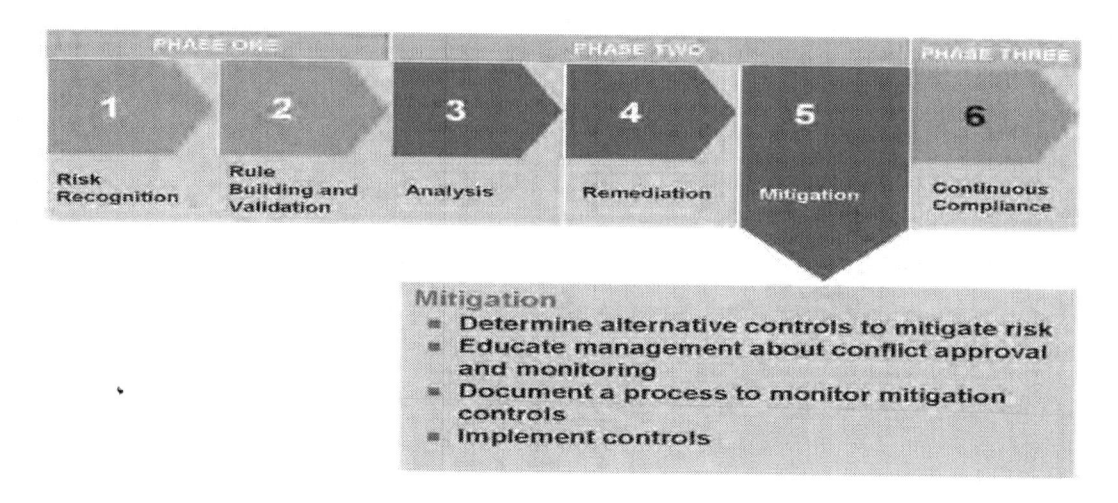

20) Which of the following statements are not true regarding Mitigation Phase?

   a. Implement controls
   b. Determine alternatives for making risks
   c. Document a process to monitor mitigation controls
   d. Educate management about conflict approval and monitoring

Answer: b

Explanation:

SoD Risk Management Process Phase Two: Mitigation
The purpose of the mitigation phase is to determine what mitigation controls are needed for those duties that cannot be segregated.

Phase Two: Mitigation

PHASE ONE | PHASE TWO | PHASE THREE
1 Risk Recognition | 2 Rule Building and Validation | 3 Analysis | 4 Remediation | 5 Mitigation | 6 Continuous Compliance

Mitigation
- Determine alternative controls to mitigate risk
- Educate management about conflict approval and monitoring
- Document a process to monitor mitigation controls
- Implement controls

21) Which of the following are the different types of mitigation controls?

Note: There is more than one correct answer to the question

a. Preventative controls
b. Detective controls
c. Reactive controls
d. Recursive controls

Answer: a, b

Explanation:

Types of Mitigation Controls
There are two types of mitigation controls:
- **Preventative controls** Minimize the likelihood or impact of a risk before it actually occurs.
- **Detective controls** Alert when a risk takes place and enables the responsible person to initiate corrective measures.

Preventative	Detective
Configuration	Activity Reports
Custom Objects	Budget Review
User Exits	Plan vs. Actual Reviews
Security	Technical Logs
Workflow	Alerts
...	...

22) Which of the following steps are required for setting up mitigation control?

Note: There is more than one correct answer to the question

a. Naming conventions for controls
b. Approval
c. Monitor
d. Assignment to roles and users

Answer: a, b, c, d

Explanation:

Setting up Mitigation Controls: Overview

Required steps:
• Naming convention for controls
• Definition: Who / what / how often / why (control objective)
• Approval: The person who is responsible for approving setup of mitigation controls, for example, the Sarbanes-Oxley Act team
• Monitors: The person who is in charge of performing the mitigation control
• Assignment to roles
• Assignment to users

23) Which of the following person is responsible for monitoring the use of actions and permissions associated with the risk?

    a. Approver
    b. Monitor
    c. Risk Owner
    d. Administrator

Answer: c

Explanation:

Definition of responsibilities:
Approver
    - Approve the control and identify appropriate mitigation monitors.
    - Ensure monitors are executing applicable controls within the period frequency stated in a mitigation control.
Monitor
    Perform the actions identified in the control to monitor users and identify inappropriate actions.
Risk owner
    Responsible for monitoring the use of actions and permissions associated with a risk
• Create business units and assign monitors to each.

24) In which of the following scenarios alerts are used?

    a. As a temporary mitigation control
    b. Accessing critical actions
    c. Accessing multiple conflicting actions
    d. All of the above

Answer: d

Explanation:

Alerts: Overview

Alerts are used for the following scenarios:
- As a temporary mitigation control
- To display users accessing multiple conflicting actions
- To display users accessing critical actions
- To ensure effectiveness of mitigation control by showing delays in starting mitigation reports

25) In which of the following conditions, a role or user appears?

   Note: There is more than one correct answer to the question

   a. Validity date is not within the range
   b. User account has expired
   c. User has been deleted
   d. Role has been deleted

Answer: a, b, c, d

Explanation:

Invalid Mitigation Controls the Invalid Mitigation Controls report is available from both the user and role-risk-analysis features within the Informer tab. When this new report type is selected, a validity date field appears, which defaults to the current date.

A given role or user appears if any of the following conditions exists:
- The validity date is not within the range associated with the mitigating control assignment.
- The user account has expired or has been deleted.
- The role has been deleted.
- The user or role no longer contains the risk.

You can find the Invalid Mitigation Controls report by choosing *Informer → Risk Analysis → Role Level* or *Informer → Risk Analysis → User Level*
Report Type = Invalid Mitigating Controls

26) Which of the following statements are true regarding SoD violations from custom programs?

   Note: There is more than one correct answer to the question

   a. It is useful when customizing a rule set
   b. Two types of report critical actions and conflicting actions available
   c. Custom programs can be built using Z transactions
   d. Report type is available in Summary and Detail Version

Answer: a, b, c, d

Explanation:

SoD Violations from Custom Programs the SoD Violations from Custom Programs report is useful when customizing a rule set. Often, clients will build custom "Z" transactions that contain calls to SAP transactions. If those SAP transactions are critical or are SoD-relevant, the" transaction may need to be included in the rule set. The report can also be executed against standard programs.

There are two report types:
- Any critical action in any program
- Conflicting actions in one program

Each report type is available in both a Summary and a Detail version. You can select the desired report type of the selection criteria screen, and when a report is displayed you can switch to the alternate version by choosing the *Summary* or *Detail* buttons.
You can access this report by choosing *Informer → Audit Reports → Miscellaneous*.

Risk Terminator

27) **Which of the following necessary settings are required when implementing the Risk Terminator?**

    Note: There is more than one correct answer to the question

    a. Select the CC release to be used
    b. RFC destination for release
    c. PFCG plugin

d. PFCG user assignment plug in
e. SU01 Role Assignment

Answer: a, b, c, d, e

Explanation:

Risk Terminator There are some necessary configuration settings when implementing Risk Terminator. You need to make these settings before Risk Terminator will work. Start transaction /n/VIRSA/ZRTCNFG to configure Risk Terminator.

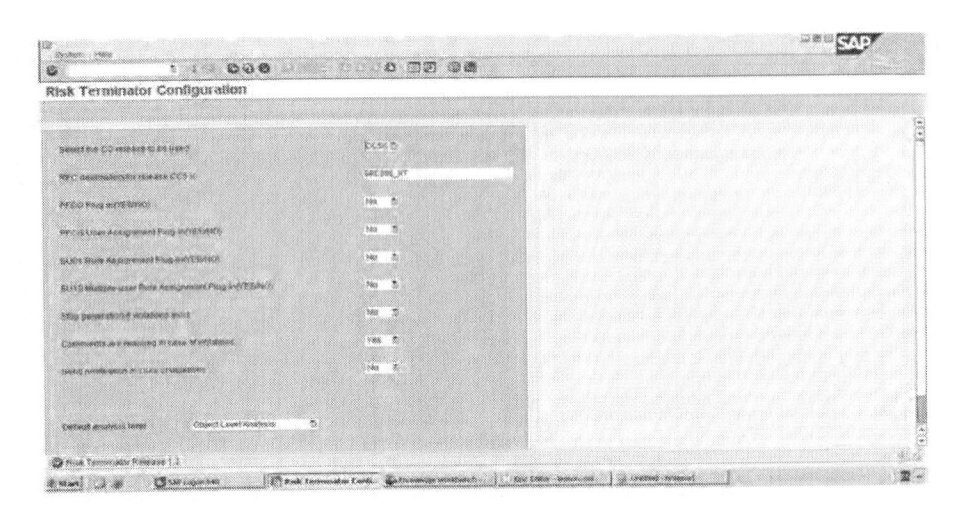

Select the CC release to be used in this scenario; we use Risk Analysis and Remediation 5.3 to connect to Risk Terminator.

RFC destination for release CC5.X This RFC is required so that Risk Terminator can run a risk analysis when a role is developed or a user's master record is modified.

PFCG Plugin (Yes/No) if you set this parameter to *Yes*, it will analyze changes that occur through PFCG, such as new roles that are created and roles that are modified.

PFCG user assignment Plug-in (Yes/No) With this setting set to *Yes*, if you make a user assignment through PFCG, Risk Terminator will analyze the user's access with the new role assigned and determine if there are any new risks involved.

SU01 Role assignment (Yes/No) if this is set to *yes*; Risk Terminator will analyze role assignment through SU01 and determine if there are any new SoD violations generated from that change.

SU10 Multiple-user Role assignment Plug-in (Yes/No) If this is set to *Yes* when you make changes under SU10, Risk Terminator will analyze those Changes. This is also helpful because mass changes through SU10 could produce SoD conflicts with users through mass maintenance changes.

Stop generation if violations exist this setting will stop any role generation if there are risks generated by any change or transaction codes that are introduced to the role.

Caution: When activating stop generation, be mindful on which system (QA, DEV, or PROD) it should be activated. If it is activated for all, it can impact the security team's response time to making changes to roles or creating new roles.

Comments are required in case of violations. If this is set to *yes*, a *Comments* screen will appear if there are SoD violations during the risk analysis of a new role, or a role change.

Send notification in case of violations

28) Which of the following statements are true regarding Uploading Initial Data?

   Note: There is more than one correct answer to the question

   a. It is default system data prepackaged with the system
   b. It is imported directly from the application itself
   c. It needs to be imported only when it was not during post installation step of SAP BO Access control
   d. Initial data upload can be verified

Answer: a, b, c, d

Explanation:

Uploading Initial Data Before you begin configuring Compliant User Provisioning, you must import initial system data. This data is the default system data that is prepackaged with the system. It is the minimum set of data required for the application to function properly and is imported directly from the application itself.

Caution: Import initial data only if it was not done during the post-installation phase of the SAP Business Objects Access Control installation process.
You can verify that the initial data was already imported by checking if there are request types on the main request page for users.

Verification of Initial Data Upload

Procedure to Upload Initial Data
- On the *Configuration* tab, choose *Initial System Data*. The *Initialize DB* screen appears.
- Choose *Browse*.
- Navigate to the directory containing the Compliant User Provisioning installation files.
- In the *Browse* window, double-click the appropriate XML file.

There are three options for import: (1) Insert, (2) Append, and (3) Clean and Insert. Each delivered initial load file will specify how to load.

- The files to import are:
AE_init_append_data.xml – Select *Append*.
AE_init_append_data_ForSODUARReview.xml – Select *Append*.
AE_init_clean_and_insert_data.xml – Select *Clean and Insert*.
- Choose *Import...*

User Data Source

29) Which of the following are the different types of User data sources are available?

   a. Using UME as user data source
   b. Using LDAP as user data source
   c. Using multiple data sources as user data source
   d. All of the above

Answer: d

Explanation:

User Data Source Use the *User Data Source* option to increase the scope of SAP back-end systems that you configured in the *Connectors* screen. Define the primary source for extracting user data on the *User Data Source* screen. Mapping the data source allows Compliant User Provisioning to search for all users, managers, and approvers. However, keep in mind that this is not an authorization mechanism to check for existing users and managers.

The data source that you map (such as LDAP, SAPHR, SAP, or SAPUME) also determines how certain types of data are handled through the assigned protocols and from specific systems. Therefore, once you select a user data source, you do not need to perform any additional configuration to map the user ID.

30) Which of the following data source is most common data source to find user and approver data in an enterprise portal environment?

   a. Using UME as user data source
   b. Using LDAP as user data source
   c. Using multiple data sources as user data source
   d. All of the above

Answer: a

Explanation:

• **Using UME as the user data source:** The SAP UME is the most common data source to find user and approver data in an enterprise portal environment. UME is also used a data source by SAP Net Weaver for other applications that are integrated into the SAP system. The SAP UME is a central management repository for retrieving SAP user data through Compliant User Provisioning.

- **Using LDAP as the user data source:** Using LDAP as the user data source is preferable, because LDAP is normally the first point of entry for users accessing the enterprise system. LDAPs generally contain as much information about the user as the SAP business system. If you set the user detail data source to LDAP, the user's manager listed on the LDAP record can automatically populate the request during the request creation.

- **Using multiple data sources as the user details data source:** When you select *Multiple Data sources*, the *Multiple Data sources* screen appears, and you can select the systems involved with the search. You can also order the sequence in which the data sources should be searched. Compliant User Provisioning searches the systems in the specified order until it finds the user ID and retrieves the user's details from that system.

For example, all employee user information can be fetched from SAP HCM. However, part-time and contract personnel detail information exists in an LDAP system. In this case, you can configure multiple data sources with SAP HCM and LDAP systems which fetch detail information for both employees and contractors.

31) Compliant User provisioning supports multiple data sources for which of the following system types?

   Note: There is more than one correct answer to the question

   a. SAP
   b. SAP HR
   c. ORAAPPS
   d. PEOPLESOFT

Answer: a, b, c, d

Explanation:

Connecting Compliant User Provisioning to a Back-End System
After installing Compliant User Provisioning, you must configure the interactions with the appropriate back-end systems via connectors. This is essential to provision approved users to the back-end systems. Compliant User Provisioning supports several connector types for back-end systems.

Connectors facilitate the transfer of data between Compliant User Provisioning and SAP systems, non-SAP systems, SAP Enterprise Portal, LDAP, and other systems. By configuring the connectors, you specify how Compliant User Provisioning communicates with these back-end systems.
Compliant User Provisioning supports multiple data sources where you can define data sources, including their sequence order for extracting data. The supported multiple data sources include the following system types:

- SAP
- SAPHR

- LDAP
- JDE (JD Edwards)
- SAPEP (SAP Enterprise Portal)
- ORAAPPS (Oracle Applications)
- PEOPLESOFT

For multiple LDAPs, Compliant User Provisioning supports:

- Microsoft Active Directory
- Sun Microsystems Sun One
- Novell E-Directory
- IBM Tivoli
- Any other LDAP supported in SAP Net Weaver

32) **Which of the following Items can be exported or imported using Compliant User provisioning?**

   Note: There is more than one correct answer to the question

   a. Initial Data
   b. Roles
   c. Connectors
   d. HR Triggers
   e. Workflow configuration

Answer: a, b, c, d, e

Explanation:

Exporting and Importing Configuration Settings Compliant User Provisioning now supports the export and import of configuration settings. This is not a transport mechanism to move changes from the development system to production, but can be used to create a production system for the first time by making a copy of the development system.

Exporting Configuration Settings

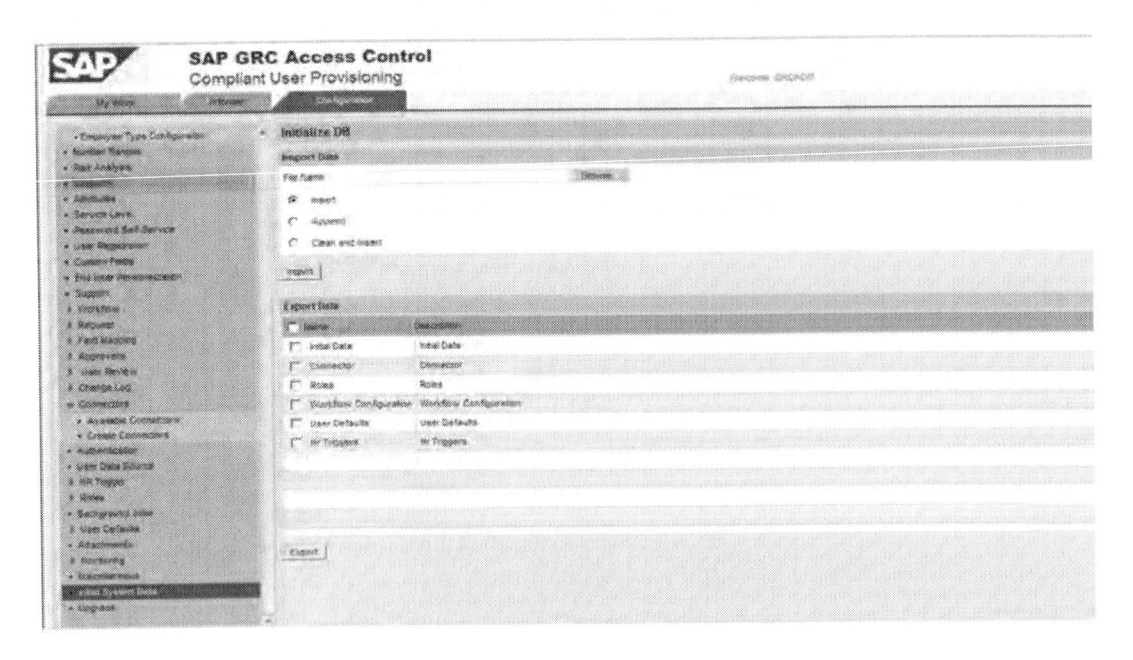

Items that can be exported or imported:
- Initial Data
- Connectors
- Roles
- Workflow Configuration
- User Defaults
- HR Triggers

33) **Which of the following are the basic components of a workflow in Compliant User provisioning?**

   Note: There is more than one correct answer to the question

   a. Initiator
   b. Stage
   c. Path
   d. Clause

Answer: a, b, c

Explanation:

Workflow in Compliant User Provisioning

Compliant User Provisioning is an automated end-to-end user request, approval, and compliant provisioning solution that is Web-based and workflow configurable with proactive SoD compliance checking

End-to-end automation means that sequences can be automatically triggered based on events such as a new employee hire or a job change, then processed through dynamic workflow, and finally provisioned directly into multiple systems. These steps can be performed by business users without any involvement from IT or application security personnel.

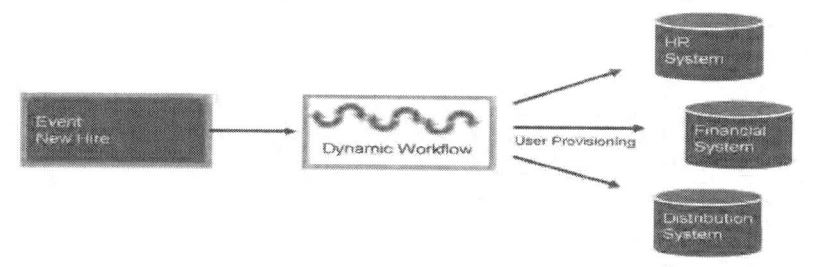

Components of a Workflow
A workflow in Compliant User Provisioning is made up of three basic components: the initiator, the stage, and the path.

34) Suppose a three stage workflow is initiated in the request then which of the following component triggers the workflow?

- a. Initiator
- b. Stage
- c. Path
- d. Clause

Answer: a

Explanation:

Every workflow is started by a unique initiator that is defined in the request. The following figures show an example of a three-stage workflow.

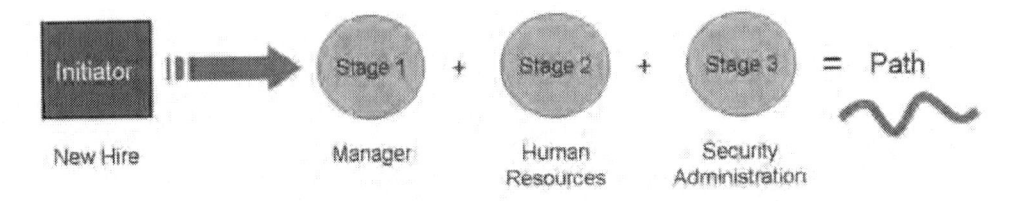

- Initiator: Triggers workflow
- Stage: A single step in the workflow that identifies an approver or group approvers for the requested access
- Path: A grouping of multiple stages, in the order they should be executed, to form a complete approval workflow cycle for an access request initiator

35) Which of the following statement is not true related to Approver determinators of a stage?

   a. Purpose of a stage is to pass a request to an approve
   b. Triggering the workflow
   c. Approver determinators defines and identifies the approver of a stages
   d. Several predefined standards are delivered with compliant User provisioning

Answer: b

Explanation:

Approver Determinators for a Stage
The primary purpose of any stage is to pass a request to an approver. When you create a stage, you define the user who must approve or deny a request when the request reaches that stage. When you define a stage, you specify the approver for that stage. The term "approver determinators" defines the approvers for the request and identifies the approver(s) of the stage. You can choose from several approver determinators on any stage. These are all delivered standard with Compliant User Provisioning.

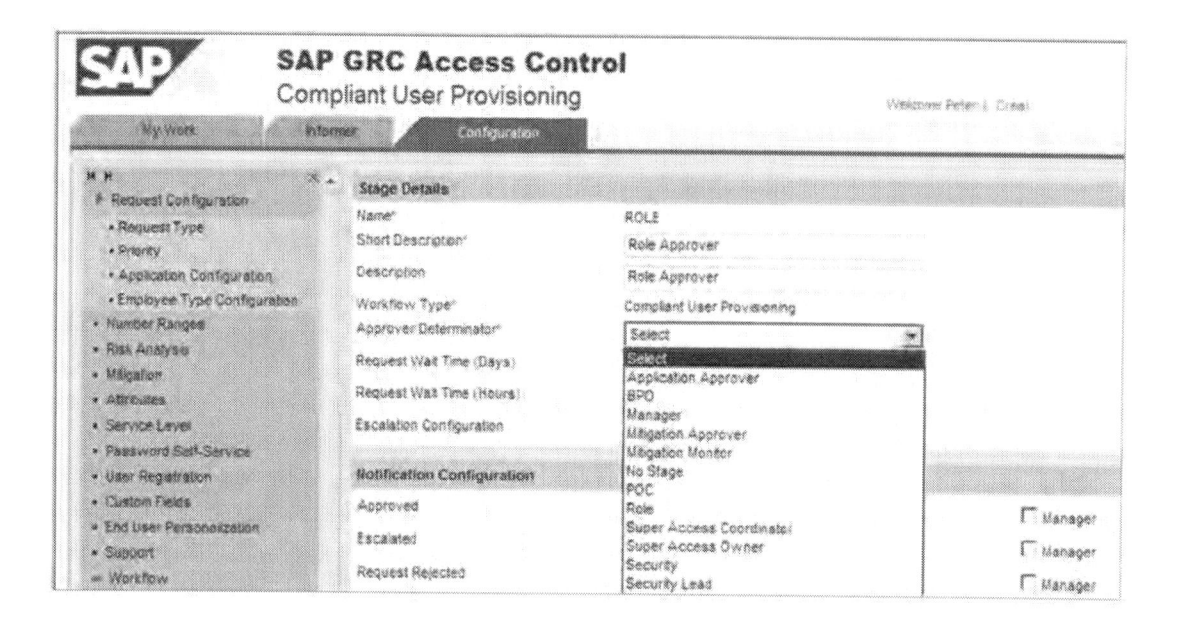

36) Which of the following different configuration areas available that can be added to a stage?

Note: There is more than one correct answer to the question

a. Notification Configuration
b. Additional Security configuration
c. Additional configuration
d. Approval Reaffirm

Answer: a, b, c, d

Explanation:

Stage Customizing Options There are various optional configurations you can add to a stage to specify notifications, require risk analysis, and manage security. When you configure a stage, you determine which options apply.

There are three configuration areas:

• Notification Configuration
• Additional Configuration
• Additional Security Configuration (Approval Reaffirm)

Note: If the user, requestor, and approver are the same, each receives multiple e-mail notifications. When sending an e-mail notification to the user and the requestor if the user is the requestor, the system sends two e-mail notifications. If the requestor and the manager are the same user, that person receives two e-mails

37) Which of the following different actions are possible for Notification Configuration?

Note: There is more than one correct answer to the question

a. Approved
b. Rejected
c. Escalation
d. Next Approver

Answer: a, b, c, d

Explanation:

Notification Configuration The *Notification Configuration* screen configures e-mail notifications for a stage to determine whether and to whom the system sends notifications about the actions taken at this stage. There are four possible actions:

1. Approved: The system sends the e-mail notification configured on the *Approved* tab when the approver approves the request.

2. Rejected: The system sends the e-mail notification configured on the *Rejected* tab when the approver rejects or denies the request.

3. Escalation: The system sends the e-mail notification configured on the *Escalation* tab when the approver fails to respond to the request within the allotted wait time and an escalation has occurred.

4. Next Approver: The system sends the e-mail notification to the approver(s) of the stage when the request enters this stage. The next approver is the approver of the current stage

38) Which of the following actions that can be configured to require reaffirmation?

Note: There is more than one correct answer to the question

a. Approve
b. Reject
c. Create user
d. Delete user

Answer: a, b, c

Explanation:

Additional Security Configuration the *Additional Security Configuration* screen specifies whether the approver needs to confirm his or her identity to take an action at this stage. Approvers confirm their identities (reaffirm their decisions) by entering their password at a prompt when they take an action.

The actions that can be configured to require reaffirmation are:

- Approve
- Reject
- Create User

39) In which of the following other areas workflow Functionality can be used?

   Note: There is more than one correct answer to the question

   a. Risk Maintenance
   b. Control Maintenance
   c. User maintenance
   d. Role Maintenance

Answer: a, b, c, d

Explanation:

Other Areas of Workflow Functionality

SAP Business Objects Access Control Compliant User Provisioning can be used for:

- Risk maintenance
- Control maintenance
- Mitigation activities
- User maintenance
- Role maintenance
- Requesting super user access

Streamlined User Access Management

40) Which of the following are the key benefits of Streamlined User Access Management?

Note: There is more than one correct answer to the question

   a. Reduces Manual Task
   b. Faster and Easier
   c. Less Security
   d. Improved security

Answer: a, b, d

Explanation:

Access Control standardizes on SAP Business workflow technology and supports more flexible and tailored access request and approver views, simplifying the provisioning process.

Key Benefits

Business workflow reduces manual tasks and streamlines access request processing
Leverage existing resources for workflow administration and configuration
Faster and easier for users to request the roles they need
Utilize existing HR structure for automated and compliant position-based role assignment
Improved security and richer request context

41) Which of the following is the new workflow functionality in SAP Business Objects AC 10.0?

Note: There is more than one correct answer to the question

   a. One process ID can have multiple requests
   b. Process ID are disabled
   c. Initiator rule is able to trigger multiple paths
   d. Improved security

Answer: a, c

Explanation:

Workflow Key Terms in SAP Business Objects AC 10.0 Mapping Previous Workflow Terms to the New Workflow Functionality

One process ID can have multiple request types Access Request: Create Request, Change Request, etc.

Function Approval: Update Function, Delete Function, etc.

One initiator rule is able to trigger multiple paths based on the rule result value

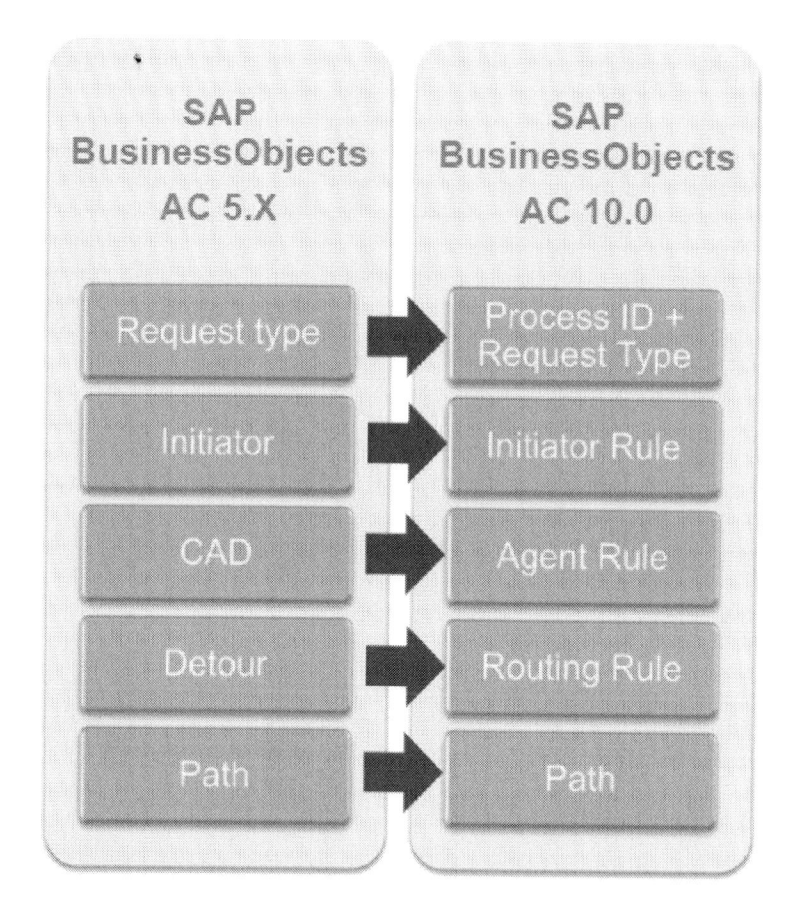

SAP BusinessObjects AC 5.X	SAP BusinessObjects AC 10.0
Request type	Process ID + Request Type
Initiator	Initiator Rule
CAD	Agent Rule
Detour	Routing Rule
Path	Path

Configuring MSMP Workflows

42) Which of the following is the pre configuration that needs to be completed before configuring MSMP workflows?

   a. Activate Event Linkage
   b. Number ranges for access requests to be defined
   c. Automatic workflow customizing
   d. All of the above

Answer: d

Explanation:

Prerequisites: The following configuration should have been completed as part of the initial post-installation steps:

GRC_MSMP_CONFIGURATIONBC Set has been enabled

Perform Automatic Workflow Customizing

Perform Tasks Specific Customizing

Activate Event Linkage

Define number ranges for Access Requests

Connectors assigned to the PROV integration scenario

43) Which of the following role is required to approve for Access request and user access review?

   a. SAP_GRAC_ACCESS_APPROVER
   b. SAP_GRAC_ACCESS_CONTROLLER
   c. SAP_GRAC_MSMP_WF_ADMIN_ALL
   d. None of the above

Answer: a

Explanation:

You need at least the admin for configuration, an approver and a standard business user for request creation.

For workflow maintenance:

SAP_GRAC_MSMP_WF_ADMIN_ALLAdministrator role for MSMP workflow
SAP_GRAC_MSMP_WF_CONFIG_ALLConfiguration role for MSMP workflows

For workflow management:

SAP_GRAC_ACCESS_APPROVER Approver for Access Request and User Access Review
SAP_GRAC_CONTROL_APPROVER Approver for Control Maintenance and Assignments requests
SAP_GRAC_SUPER_USER_MGMT_OWNER Approver for Firefighter Log
SAP_GRAC_FUNCTION_APPROVER Approver for Function Maintenance
SAP_GRAC_RISK_OWNER Approver for Risk Maintenance and SoD Risk Review
SAP_GRAC_ROLE_MGMT_ROLE_OWNER Approver for Role Maintenance

Maintain MSMP Workflows

44) Which of the following setting are configured in Process Global settings in Maintain MSMP workflows?

   a. Process Ids Configured
   b. Escape conditions
   c. Notification settings
   d. All of the above

Answer: d

Explanation:

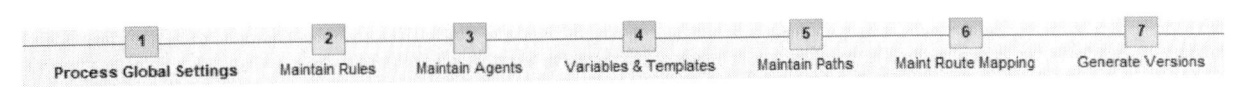

1. Process Global Settings — 2. Maintain Rules — 3. Maintain Agents — 4. Variables & Templates — 5. Maintain Paths — 6. Maint Route Mapping — 7. Generate Versions

In this step settings that apply to all process IDs are configured, such as escape conditions and notifications settings

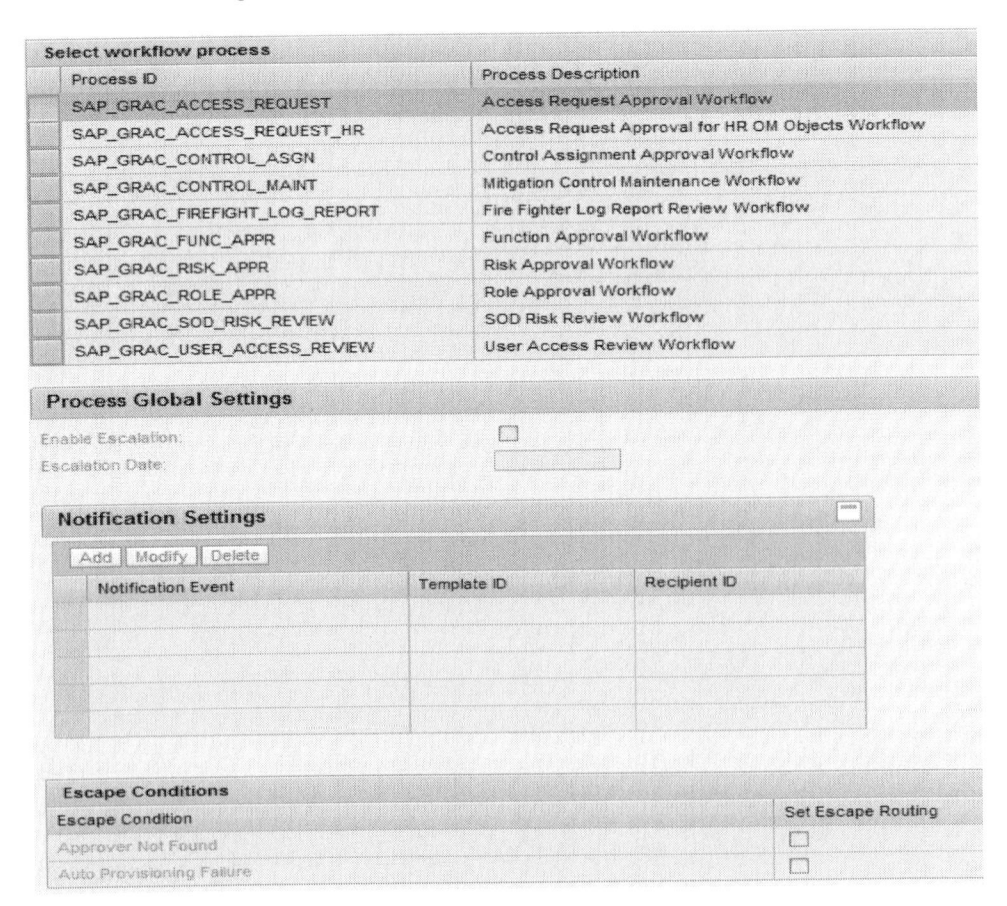

Select workflow process

Process ID	Process Description
SAP_GRAC_ACCESS_REQUEST	Access Request Approval Workflow
SAP_GRAC_ACCESS_REQUEST_HR	Access Request Approval for HR OM Objects Workflow
SAP_GRAC_CONTROL_ASGN	Control Assignment Approval Workflow
SAP_GRAC_CONTROL_MAINT	Mitigation Control Maintenance Workflow
SAP_GRAC_FIREFIGHT_LOG_REPORT	Fire Fighter Log Report Review Workflow
SAP_GRAC_FUNC_APPR	Function Approval Workflow
SAP_GRAC_RISK_APPR	Risk Approval Workflow
SAP_GRAC_ROLE_APPR	Role Approval Workflow
SAP_GRAC_SOD_RISK_REVIEW	SOD Risk Review Workflow
SAP_GRAC_USER_ACCESS_REVIEW	User Access Review Workflow

Process Global Settings

Enable Escalation:
Escalation Date:

Notification Settings

Add | Modify | Delete

Notification Event	Template ID	Recipient ID

Escape Conditions

Escape Condition	Set Escape Routing
Approver Not Found	
Auto Provisioning Failure	

Redelivered Process IDs:

Access Request Approval Workflow

Access Request Approval Workflow for HR OM Objects

Control Assignment Approval Workflow

Mitigation Control Maintenance Workflow

Fire Fighter Log Report Review Workflow

Function Approval Workflow

Risk Approval Workflow

Role Approval Workflow

SOD Risk Review Workflow

User Access Review Workflow

45) According to rule's objective, which of the following are the different kinds of Rule?

   Note: There is more than one correct answer to the question

   a. Initiator Rule
   b. Agents Rule
   c. Routing Rule
   d. Notification Variables Rule

Answer: a, b, c, d

Explanation:

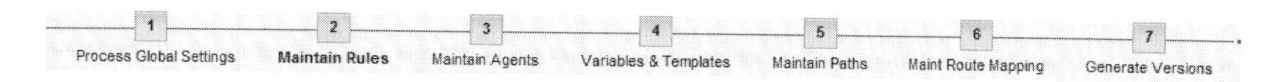

1 Process Global Settings — 2 Maintain Rules — 3 Maintain Agents — 4 Variables & Templates — 5 Maintain Paths — 6 Maint Route Mapping — 7 Generate Versions

Maintain Rules includes a list of all available rules to be used when configuring a workflow. If a new rule is created it must be added to this list. This is also where the default initiator is configured.

There are different Rule Kinds according to the rule's objective:

Initiator Rule

Agents Rule

Routing Rule

Notification Variables Rule

Rules can be coded in different ways; these are the different Rule Types:

Function Module Based Rule

ABAP Class Based Rule

BRFplus Rule

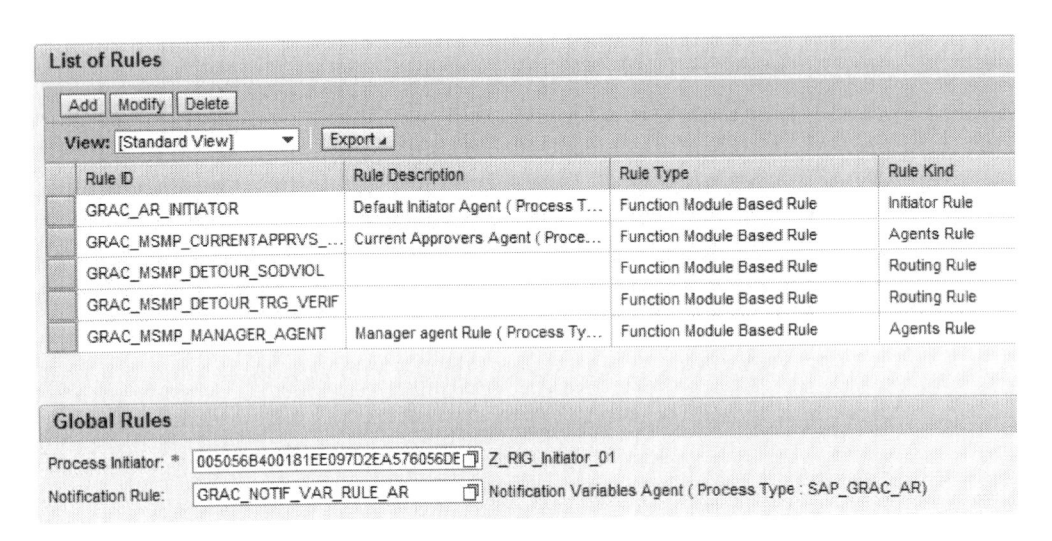

46) Which of the following rule kind determines the recipients of a stage?

    a. Initiator Rule
    b. Agents Rule
    c. Routing Rule
    d. Notification Variables Rule

Answer: b

Explanation:

Rule Kinds:

•**Initiator Rule** –determines the path upon submission of the request

•**Agents Rule** –determines the recipients of a stage

•**Routing Rule** –determines a detour routing based upon an attribute of the request (for example, Sod Violations Exist, Training Verification, No Role Owner)

•**Notification Variables Rule** –determines the variable values at runtime used in the notification e-mails.

47) Which of the following rule types defines function module that is coded to output rule results

a. BRFplus Rule
b. Function module based rule
c. ABAP class based rule
d. BRF Plus Flat Rule

Answer: b

Explanation:

Rule Types:

- **BRFplusRule**: is a rule defined in the BRFplusapplication to fetch rule results, depending on conditions inside the rule.
- **Function Module Based Rule:** Function module is coded to output rule results.
- **ABAP Class Based Rule**: ABAP Classis coded to output rule results
- **BRFplusFlat Rule (Line-item by Line-item)**: BRFplusrule which is defined for only one line item (rule will be called once for each line-item in the request) Also referred to as BRF+ Easy.

48) Which of following are the different agents types can be maintained in Maintain Agent step?

Note: There is more than one correct answer to the question

a. API Rules
b. Directly Mapped users
c. PFCG Roles
d. User groups

Answer: a, b, c, d

Explanation:

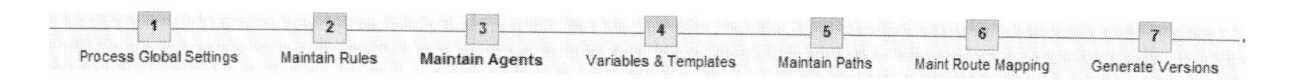

1. Process Global Settings
2. Maintain Rules
3. Maintain Agents
4. Variables & Templates
5. Maintain Paths
6. Maint Route Mapping
7. Generate Versions

A list of all available agents for a workflow is maintained in step 3. Agents have a type and a purpose assigned.

Agents

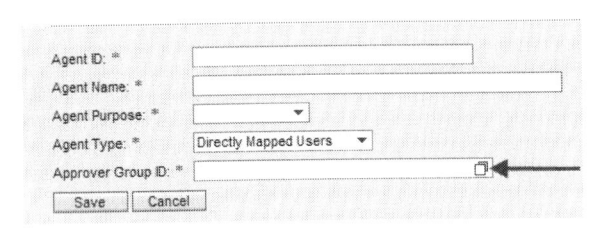

Agent ID	Agent Name	Agent Type	Agent Purpose
GRAC_MANAGER	Manager	GRC API Rules	Approval
GRAC_MANAGER_NOTIFICATION	Manager - Notification	GRC API Rules	Notification
GRAC_OTHER_APPROVERS	Other approvers	GRC API Rules	Notification
GRAC_POINT_CONTACT	Point of contact	GRC API Rules	Approval
GRAC_REQUESTER	Requester	GRC API Rules	Notification

Agent Purpose

Notification: Recipients for email

Approval: Recipients to process request

Agent Types

API Rules, coded as per rule's type

Directly Mapped Users

PFCG Roles, and

User Groups

49) Which of the following agent type allows us to define the static user groups?

    a. API Rules
    b. Directly Mapped users
    c. PFCG Roles
    d. User groups

Answer: b

Explanation:

Directly Mapped Users allows you to define static user groups

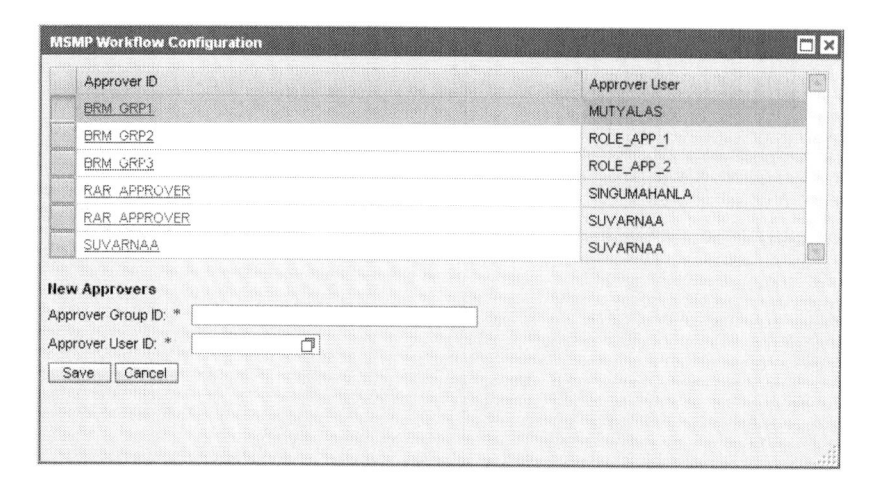

50) Which of the following agent types determines the recipient of a workflow based on a rule or a user group assignment?

Note: There is more than one correct answer to the question

a. API Rules
b. Directly Mapped users
c. PFCG Roles
d. User groups

Answer: c, d

Explanation:

Below two agent types will determine the recipients of a workflow based on a role or a user group assignment

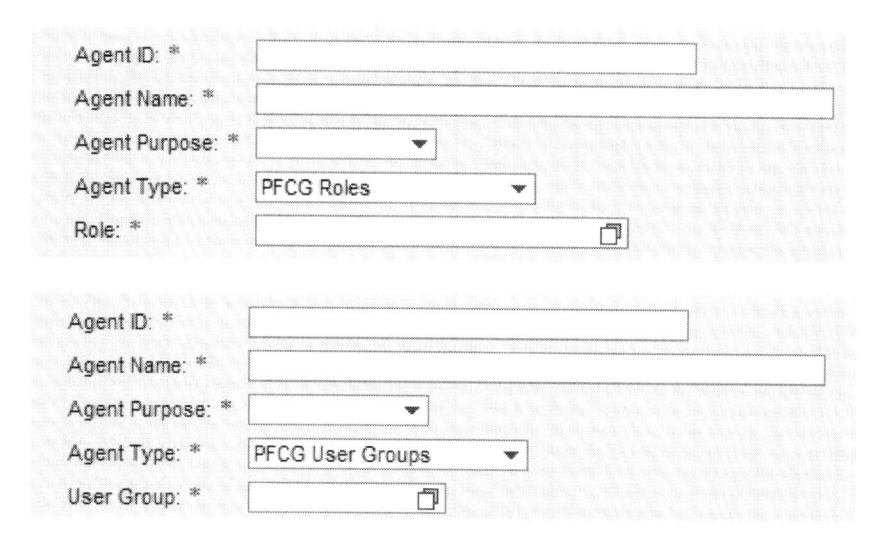

51) Which of the following agent type will determine the recipients based on the rule maintained in Maintain Rule step while configuring MSMP workflows?

   a. GRC API Rules
   b. Directly Mapped users
   c. PFCG Roles
   d. User groups

Answer: a

Explanation:

API Rule agent type will determine the recipients based on a rule maintained in step Maintain Rule.

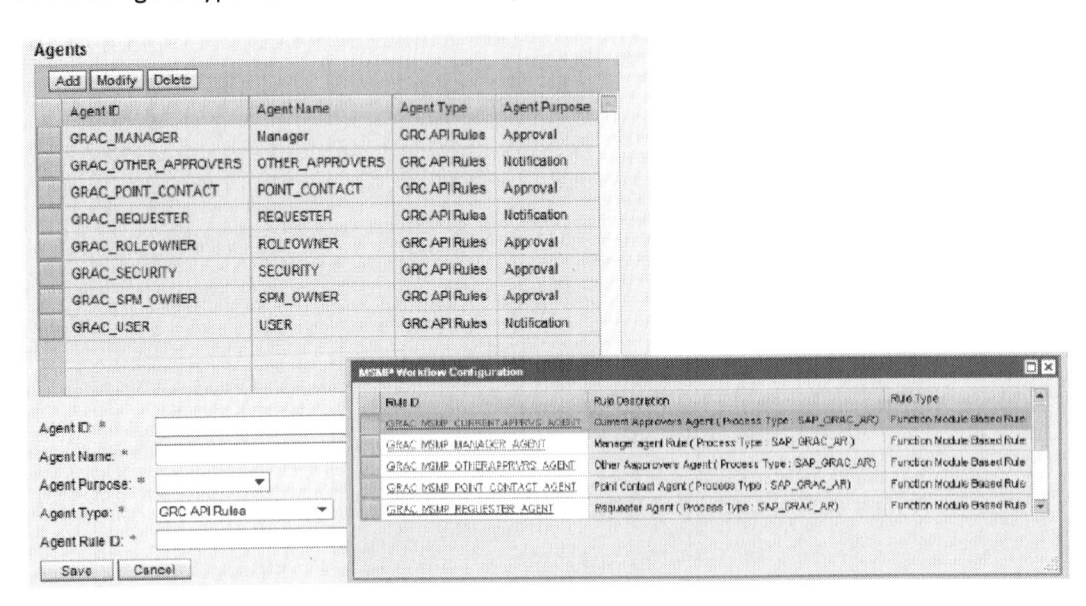

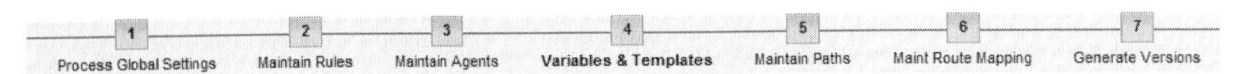

52) In which of the following step email notifications are maintained while configuring MSMP workflows?

   a. Process Global settings
   b. Maintain Rules
   c. Variables and Templates
   d. Maintain Route Mapping

Answer: c

Explanation:

In this step all templates for email notifications are maintained. The templates are created using transaction SE61.

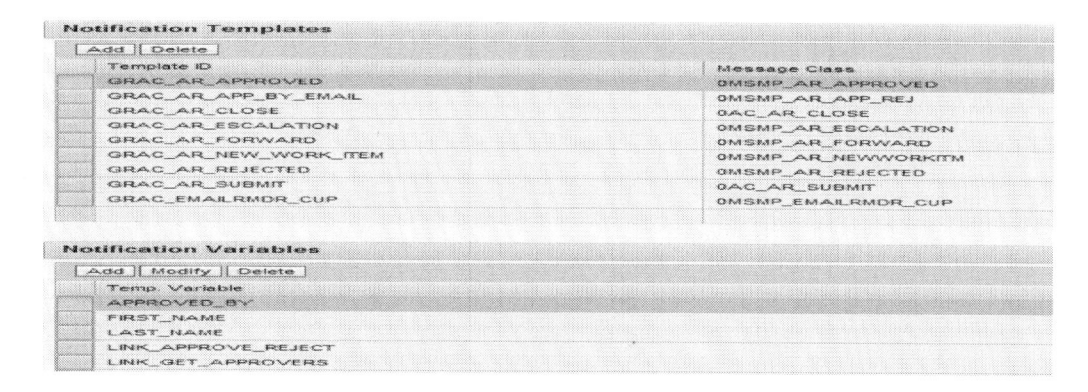

Notifications can be sent on different events, such as:
New Work Item
Approval
Rejection
Escalation
Request submission
Request closure
Reminder

53) In which of the following step mapping between rule results and paths to route the requests while configuring MSMP workflow?

    a. Process Global settings
    b. Maintain Rules
    c. Variables and Templates
    d. Maintain Route Mapping

Answer: d

Explanation:

Maintain Route Mapping step you define the mapping between rule results and paths to route the requests .Always the Global Initiator must be used; if multiple paths are required the Global Initiator must return different result values
Routing rules for detours can be added here as well

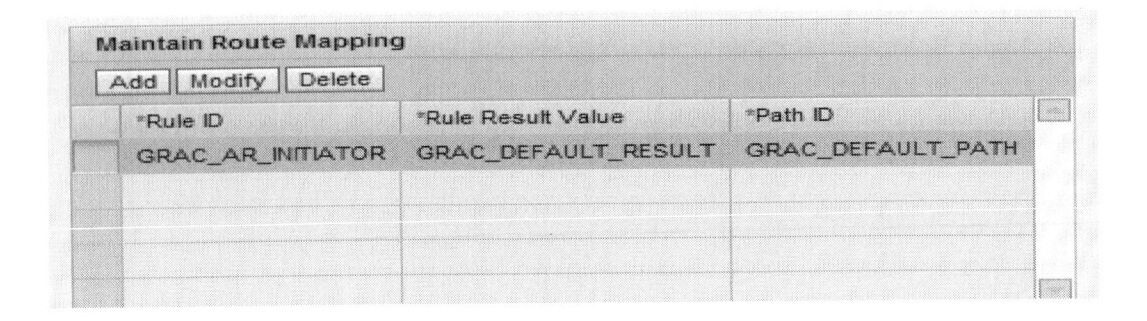

54) Which of the following activities are needed for creating Function Module Rule?

    a. Function group creation
    b. Workflow defining
    c. Maintaining Function module
    d. All of the above

Answer: d

Explanation:

Function Module rules allow developers to create complex rules by using ABAP Code. These are the activities needed for creating a FM rule:

Create Function Group in SE37: Function Modules will be added to the group
Define Workflow Related MSMP Rules: For generating the FM rule content from a template before maintaining it.
Maintain Function Module in SE37: For maintaining the FM rule contents.

```
Access Control
  • Maintain Configuration Settings
  • Maintain Mapping for Actions and Connector Groups
  • Maintain Connector Settings
  • Maintain Plug-in Settings
  • Maintain Criticality Levels for Superuser Management
  • Distribute Jobs for Parallel Processing
  • Maintain Access Risk Levels
  • Maintain Business Processes and Subprocesses
  • Maintain AC Applications and BRFplus Function Mapping
  • Maintain Data Sources Configuration
  • Maintain Custom User Group
  • Maintain Master User ID Mapping
  • Maintain Exclude Objects for Batch Risk Analysis
  Workflow for Access Control
    • Activate Event Linkage for AC Workflows
    • Activate MSMP Content for AC
    • Maintain MSMP Workflows
    • Generate MSMP Process Versions
    • Define Workflow-Related MSMP Rules
    • Define Business Rule Framework
    • Maintain Notification Messages
```

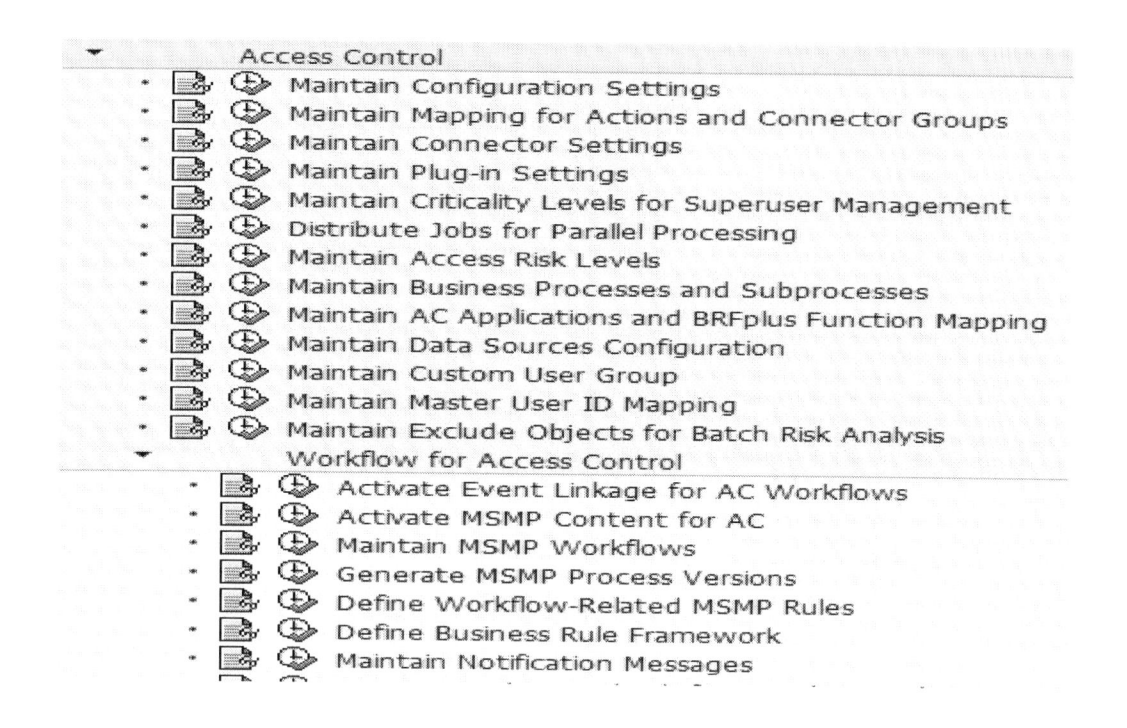

Workflow configuration for Change Management

55) Suppose you are configuring workflow for change management then which of the following workflow components must be setup?

Note: There is more than one correct answer to the question

    a. Activating request types
    b. Activating mitigation URL settings
    c. Creating paths
    d. Creating stages
    e. Creating workflow initiators

Answer: a, b, c, d, e

Explanation:

Configuring Workflow for Change Management
The delivered workflow configuration options in Compliant User Provisioning include request types and Web services. These must be activated and applied in the proper settings. The rest of workflow configuration must be set up and tested by the designated application administrators.

Workflow components that must be set up in the Compliant User Provisioning *Configuration* tab for risk and mitigation control changes include:

- Activating request types:
  – Create / Update / Delete Mitigation Control
  – Create / Update / Delete Mitigation Object
  – Create / Update / Delete Risk
- Activating mitigation URL settings
- Activating mitigation and risk workflows in miscellaneous
- Creating workflow initiators for risk and mitigation changes
- Creating custom approver determinators for risk and mitigation changes
- Creating stages for risk and mitigation changes
- Creating paths for risk and mitigation changes

User Access Review

56) Which of the following are the benefits of configuring the workflow for user access review?

Note: There is more than one correct answer to the question

a. Compliance to SOX act
b. Process streamlined
c. High throughput
d. More efficient

Answer: a, b

Explanation:

User Access Review: Process Overview Managers and role approvers use User Access Review (UAR) to automate the periodic process of reviewing and reaffirming end-user role assignments. The system notifies managers to review their direct reports access to applications. Approvers must review the list of user role assignments and determine if the user still needs those roles based on their current responsibilities. Approvers either approve or remove the roles that are assigned to each user.
If the user no longer requires a role, the role is de-provisioned from back-end systems automatically or manually. If the reviewer does not complete the review in the defined period, the process can be escalated. Escalation could include the deactivation of a user's account until the review is completed.

Highlights of this process include:

- Automated decentralized user access review by business managers or role owners
- Reports generated automatically based on the company's internal control policy
- Workflow-request-based review and approval process
- Automatic de-provisioning for role removal
- Audit trail and reports for review details
- Allow manager to approve or remove roles based on employee's business function

Benefits:

- Streamline the internal control process with collaboration among business managers, internal control team, and IT team
- Provide efficiency and visibility to a company's Sarbanes-Oxley Act compliance

57) Which of the following steps are required for configuring Workflow for User access Review?

Note: There is more than one correct answer to the question

a. Activate and configure workflow
b. Setup User review options

c. Email reminder defining
   d. Scheduling of background job

Answer: a, b, c, d

Explanation:

Configuring Workflow for User Access Review

- Activate and configure UAR workflow.
− Define an initiator.
− Define a stage (one stage for reviewer and another stage for security).
− Define a path (one path for a reviewer and another path for security).
− Define a detour with condition (for role removals).
- Set up User Review options for UAR in the *Configuration* tab.
− Select if Admin Review is required.
− Select the reviewers: manager or role owner.
− Define number of lines items per request.
− Select the default request type.
− Select the default priority of the request.
- Populate the Coordinator-Reviewer Relationships table if a coordinator is to be configured for the UAR.
− The coordinator is optional; it is possible to perform the review without a coordinator.
− In addition, one coordinator might have many reviewers.

Define the e-mail reminder.
- Define the service level for UAR.
- Schedule a role usage synchronization to perform the User Access Review in Enterprise Role Management.
- Schedule the UAR Review Load Data background job in Compliant User Provisioning.
- Schedule the UAR Review Update Workflow background job in Compliant User Provisioning.

Note: You can schedule new background jobs to create workflow requests for manager or risk-owner review only after all previous UAR requests are closed.

User SoD Review

58) Which of the following are the benefits of User SoD review?

Note: There is more than one correct answer to the question

   a. Real SoD management
   b. Provide efficiency
   c. Compliance to Sox act
   d. Streamlining of process

Answer: a, b

Explanation:

User SoD Review Process Overview Business managers and risk owners use the segregation of duties (SoD) review process to automate periodic reviews of SoD conflicts. Once Risk Analysis and Remediation identifies user SoD conflicts, they must be remediated to ensure Sarbanes-Oxley-Act compliance. The system uses Risk Analysis and Remediation batch analysis data to update management graphics and to generate these SoD Review workflow requests in Compliant User Provisioning.

The reviewer can either be the user's manager or the risk owner (as defined by the Rule Architect of Risk Analysis and Remediation). Once the request is created, the system sends an e-mail notification for SoD violations to the reviewer. Depending on your configuration, requests may contain unmitigated SoD conflicts only, or both unmitigated and mitigated conflicts.

Highlights of this process include:
- Automates the decentralized SoD review by business managers or risk owners
- Real-time detection of SoD violations with reports generated and submitted to reviewers
- Workflow-request-based and approval process
- Audit trail and reports for review details

Benefits:
- Real time SoD management by exception
- Streamline the internal control process with collaboration among business managers, internal control team, and IT team
- Provide efficiency and visibility to a company's internal control process

59) Which of the following are the main advantages of Compliant User provisioning?

Note: There is more than one correct answer to the question

   a. Integrated with SAP Enterprise portal

b. Automated email notifications
c. Provides comprehensive audit trial
d. Ensures audit compliance

Answer: a, b, c, d

Explanation:

The Main Advantages of Compliant User Provisioning

• Automates, accelerates, and tracks the user access request process using workflow for SAP and non-SAP systems
• User administration with integrated risk analysis and mitigation capabilities keeps the system clean
• Provides simulation in the production system for risk analysis before changes are provisioned
• Provides a comprehensive audit trail
• Flexible configuration of multiple workflow paths and workflow triggers based on the type of request
• Self-service password reset lifts another user administration burden from the support team
• User authentication from a wide range of sources, including single-sign on, LDAP, and SAP systems
• Ensures audit compliance
• Automatically provision users and roles to users in multiple SAP systems
• Automated e-mail notification to appropriate parties
• Provides numerous reports in analytical and chart views
• Integrated with SAP Enterprise Portal

60) Which of the following option is a typical workflow creation process?

a. Plan-Test-Implement-Adjust
b. Plan-Implement-test-Adjust
c. Implement-Test-Adjust
d. Adjust-Plan-Test

Answer: b

Explanation:

Workflow Creation Process Plan - Implement - Test – Adjust

Plan

Planning a workflow requires determining:
• Required workflow functionality
• Number of workflows needed
• What stages, initiators, and paths need to be created?

- Who are the required approvers?
- What will be the final provisioning?

Planning is the most critical component in the workflow process.
- Planning requires careful consideration at the start of implementation.
- The more time spent planning workflow needs, the easier the entire process.

Implement
Create workflows per planning decisions.
- Create stages and initiators.
- Create workflow paths.
- Assign stages and an initiator to each workflow path.

Test and Adjust
Test workflows.
Adjust as necessary.
- Fix existing workflows.
- Create new workflows.

61) **Which of the following options available for password sending options while configuring the Workflows?**

Note: There is more than one correct answer to the question

  a. No password sent
  b. Password sent via SMS
  c. Password sent in email
  d. Password will send as a link

Answer: a, c, d

Explanation:

Password Sending Options
Password options in e-mails can now be configured to send the password at the end of the request.

You can configure this on the *Email Reminder* screen by choosing *Configuration → Workflow → Email Reminder*.

Send Password in Mail:
- No password sent
- Password sent in the e-mail
- Password is not sent directly in the e-mail, but will be sent as a link

62) Which of the following statements are not true regarding LDAP connectivity?

   a. It is a standard for managing large user directory
   b. Compliant User provisioning cannot use LDAP
   c. Once connected to LDAP directory mapping needs to be done
   d. Field mapping defined for the LDAP directory is specific to the LDAP system

Answer: b

Explanation:

Connecting to a LDAP Lightweight Directory Access Protocol (LDAP) is a standard for managing a Large user directory. Compliant User Provisioning can use an LDAP directory to find detailed user information.
Out of the box, Compliant User Provisioning supports Microsoft Active Directory, Sun ONE, Novell eDirectory, and IBM Tivoli LDAPs.
Once connected to a LDAP directory, you have to map the user information. The LDAP Mapping option maps fields to their corresponding fields in an LDAP database. In addition, you can add fields and then map them to attributes that already exist in your enterprise's LDAP database by selecting those attributes on the *Additional Fields* screen.

The field mapping you defined for the LDAP directory is specific to the LDAP systems that you configured in the User Data Source option. The User Data Source option is where you configure one or many LDAP data sources for searching and retrieving user detail information.

63) When an approver fails to respond within the time allotted during stage definition then which of the following options are possible for escalation?

   Note: There is more than one correct answer to the question

   a. No escalation
   b. Forward to Next stage
   c. Forward to Alternate approver
   d. Forward to administrator

Answer: a, b, c, d

Explanation:

Escalations are configured at the stage level, and dictate how to handle a request when an approver fails to respond within the time allotted during stage definition.

Options for escalation are:
- **No Escalation** (default setting): Compliant User Provisioning waits for the approver's response– even after the specified wait time passes– and does not take any steps to resolve the stalled request. The approver approves or rejects the request. An administrator can manually resolve the problem by approving on behalf of the assigned approver, forwarding the request to another approver, or rerouting the request.
- **Forward to Next Stage**: Compliant User Provisioning ignores the expected approval at this stage and proceeds to the next stage in the path. If you select this option – even if the designated approver does not respond to the request– it does not prevent the request from being approved. Use caution with this option, since it allows the request to bypass the defined approvers.
- **Forward to Alternate Approver**: This provides a fallback option if the designated approver does not respond within the allotted time. Compliant User Provisioning reassigns the approver. Alternate approvers must be maintained for the approver determinators of the stage where this option is set. Escalation to an alternate approver happens only once; there is no alternate approver for the alternate. After the system escalates the approval for the stage to the alternative approver, the original approver no longer has access to approve or reject the request.
- **Forward to Administrator**: If the approver fails to respond within the allotted time, Compliant User Provisioning forwards the request to the administrator. The administrator's information must be maintained on the *Configuration Support* screen for this option to work

64) Suppose a designated approver does not respond within the allotted time then which of the following escalation option provides the fall back option?

    a. No Escalation
    b. Forward to Next stage
    c. Forward to Alternate approver
    d. Forward to administrator

Answer: c

Explanation:

Forward to Alternate Approver: This provides a fallback option if the designated approver does not respond within the allotted time. Compliant User Provisioning reassigns the approver. Alternate approvers must be maintained for the approver determinators of the stage where this option is set. Escalation to an alternate approver happens only once; there is no alternate approver for the alternate. After the system escalates the approval for the stage to the alternative approver, the original approver no longer has access to approve or reject the request.

65) Which of the following advanced workflow are not subsets or dependents of main workflows?

   a. Escalations
   b. Detours
   c. Rerouting
   d. Forwarding

Answer: b

Explanation:

Advance workflows include:
- Escalations
- Detours
- Rerouting
- Forwarding

Detours

Detours are standalone workflows that assume management of a request from a main workflow. Detours are not subsets or dependents of main workflows. They do not have initiators, so they cannot be triggered by a submitted request. If the state of a request meets predefined conditions, a main workflow passes control of the request to a detour workflow.

The type of event that triggers a detour is typically one that prevents a main workflow from proceeding on its defined path. If something occurs that interferes with a request, the main workflow can be configured to pass the request to a detour workflow.

For example, you can design a workflow to handle a single request that includes more than one role. If an approver denies one of the roles in the request, you might want the remainder of the request to proceed. Rather than aborting the request, you can have the main workflow transfer it to a detour workflow. The detour can then continue the approval process for the remaining roles.

Super User Privilege Management

66) Which of the following are the post steps after the implementation of SAP Business Objects Access control Super user privilege Management?

   a. Verifying RFC connection
   b. Scheduling Privilege Management background job
   c. Creating Super User
   d. All of the above

Answer: d

Explanation:

Post-Installation Steps
During Super user Privilege Management post-installation, it is important to verify that the RFC connection has been created.

1. Go to transaction SM59 and verify that the RFC connection has been created.
2. Schedule a Super user Privilege Management background job for logging (SM36>/VIRSA/ZVFATBAK).
3. Create a Super user Privilege Management ID through transaction SU01.

67) Which of the following are the different ways to use the Super user privilege management application?

   a. Allow emergency changes In the production
   b. For performing some business functions
   c. For normal changes for functional team
   d. Activating the objects

Answer: a, b

Explanation:

Super user Privilege Management Super user Privilege Management helps to eliminate super users in the production environment. There are a few ways to use the application. One is to allow emergency changes in the production environment; in this case, Super user Privilege Management provides an environment where it is monitoring the use of the system. The second way is to allow functional users to have a super user level of access to perform some business functions that are not part of their daily process, for example, month-end close.

68) Which of the following needs to be identified before using Super user privilege Management?

Note: There is more than one correct answer to the question

a. Owner
b. Controller
c. Users
d. Roles

Answer: a, b, c

Explanation

Before you use Super user Privilege management, you need to identify:

1. Who the owners of the IDs will be
2. Who the controllers will be
3. Which users will need to log on through Super user Privilege Management?

The main reason why you need to define these three types of users is because you will need the user information to enter it into Super user Privilege Management when configuration is complete. This will also aid in providing the correct role assignments for the users. The roles begin with the format /VIRSA/Z_VFAT.

69) Suppose you are implementing the Super user privilege Management then which of the following additional items needs to be considered?

Note: There is more than one correct answer to the question

a. Identifying the risks
b. Only required access is provided

c. Identifying the roles
d. Firefighter any access can be provided

Answer: a, b

Explanation:
There are a few additional items to consider when implementing Super user
Privilege Management:
- Identify what risks are going to be involved within the Firefighter ID.
- Ensure that only the necessary access is given, and not SAP_ALL, to the user ID.

Enterprise Role Management

70) **Which of the following functions can be configured in any order for configuring Enterprise Role Management?**

   Note: There is more than one correct answer to the question

   a. ERM system Logs
   b. Mass role Import
   c. Workflow management configuring
   d. Role creation methodology

Answer: a, b

Explanation:

Configuring Enterprise Role Management SAP recommends that you configure certain functions before others in Enterprise Role Management. You should configure in the following order.

1. Set up initial logon to Enterprise Role Management.
   Note: This should have been done with the system install.
2. Import initial system data.
   Note: This should have been done with the system install.
3. Define the system landscape.
4. Configure management of role attributes.
5. Configure management of condition groups.
6. Set up role creation methodology.
7. Configure management of naming conventions.
8. Configure management of organizational value mapping.
9. Configure Risk Analysis and Remediation.

10. Configure workflow management.
11. Configure Compliant User Provisioning.

You can configure the following functions in any order:
- Enterprise Role Management system logs
- Management of background jobs
- Mass role import
- Other functions

71) Which of the following different types of connectors can be included in ERM?

Note: There is more than one correct answer to the question

a. Enterprise
b. SAP
c. Non SAP
d. SAP Enterprise portal

Answer: a, b, c, d

Explanation

A system landscape is a configuration of systems where role definition, creation, testing, and risk analysis are performed. Prior to creating a landscape, you must define the systems, determine which system for which you plan to generate roles, and decide which system you plan to use for risk analysis purposes only. Then you can create a system landscape where each system is associated with the actions to be used in the role management process.

You can set up different types of connectors in Enterprise Role Management, including Enterprise, non-SAP, SAP, and SAP Enterprise Portal connectors.
• Enterprise, non-SAP, and SAP Enterprise Portal connectors are descriptive connectors used to document the landscape to which each role belongs.
• The SAP connector is a live system connector that facilitates the transfer of data between Enterprise Role Management and other SAP ABAP systems.

A system landscape is a logical grouping of systems. A landscape contains more than one system and is populated by assigning systems and then associating them with a predefined action or actions. Associating actions with a system defines which action is performed in which system within a particular landscape.

72) Which of the following role attributes can be managed?

Note: There is more than one correct answer to the question

- a. Business Process
- b. Functional Areas
- c. Custom Fields
- d. Projects and Releases

Answer: a, b, c, d

Explanation:

Role attributes are the details that define a role during the role definition and creation process. You determine values for each attribute during Enterprise Role Management configuration and then assign or input the defined attributes when you create a role.

Role attributes you can manage include:

• **Business Processes** A business process is a collection of related activities that produces something of value for your organization or business and is categorized according to the organizational structure of your enterprise. A business process can be managerial, operational, or supporting, and can be defined narrowly or broadly, depending on your business needs. When you create a role in Enterprise Role Management, the business process you assign to the role is one of the role's defining attributes and determines which sub processes you can assign to that role.

• **Business Sub processes** a business process can be divided into several business sub processes, each with its own attributes. A business process typically contains one or more sub processes.

• **Functional Areas** A functional area is a classification of processes for a department or business process. Within SAP, a functional area is used to organize certain activities within a department or business process. In Enterprise Role Management, a functional area is a role attribute used to categorize roles and define the approval and role maintenance processes. In addition, a functional area is used to filter the results of a role search, identifying only those roles associated with a specific functional area.

• **Custom Fields** Custom fields allow you to add attributes to a role that are specific to your company or organization. For example, if you want to distinguish a role by region, add a custom attribute and assign a specific region when you create the role.

• **Projects and Releases** the project or release can be a project name, release name, or release number that you want to associate with a particular role. The *Project or Release ID* field allows you to track and filter roles by project or release, based on your organization's requirements.

73) Which of the following statements is not true regarding Condition Groups?

   a. It is defined from set of role attributes
   b. It is based on role values and conditions
   c. You can associate multiple process to one condition group
   d. You can apply multiple condition groups

Answer: c

Explanation:

Configuring Management of Condition Groups A condition group is defined from a set of role attributes (such as a business process, sub process, functional area, role type, or role name) and is based on role values and conditions. After you create a condition group, the system applies it to a role creation process to override the default role creation process when the criteria from the condition group are met. You can apply multiple condition groups in one role creation process, but you cannot associate multiple processes to one condition group.

74) Which of the following functions can be performed with Enterprise role management?

   Note: There is more than one correct answer to the question

   a. Risk Analysis
   b. Risk Mitigation
   c. Transaction Usage
   d. Authorization function search

Answer: a, b, c, d

Explanation:

Configuration for Risk Analysis Integration with Risk Analysis and Remediation Enterprise Role Management works directly with Risk Analysis and Remediation to perform the following functions:

- Risk analysis
- Risk mitigation
- Authorization function search
- Transaction usage

75) Which of the following connector facilitates the transfer of data between ERM and other SAP ABAP systems?

   a. Enterprise connectors
   b. Non SAP connectors
   c. SAP Connectors
   d. SAP EP connectors

Answer: c

Explanation:

Connecting Enterprise Role Management to a Back-End System You can set up different types of connectors in Enterprise Role Management. These include Enterprise, non-SAP, SAP, and SAP EP connectors.

• Enterprise, non-SAP, and SAP EP connectors are descriptive connectors used to document the landscape to which each role belongs.

• The SAP connector is a live system connector that facilitates the transfer of data between Enterprise Role Management and other SAP ABAP systems.

When setting up a landscape, you specify how you want Enterprise Role Management to communicate with the target systems by associating the connectors with predefined actions during the landscape creation process.

Note: The actions available for you to associate the connectors with are delivered with Enterprise Role Management. You cannot create your own actions.

76) Which of the following data can be exported or imported from one ERM system to another system?

   Note: There is more than one correct answer to the question

   a. Initial Data
   b. Connector
   c. Roles
   d. HR Triggers
   e. User Defaults

Answer: a, b, c, d, e

Explanation:

Exporting and Importing Configuration Settings This feature exports configuration settings from one Enterprise Role Management system and imports them into another. You must export the settings first and then use the generated file as the import source file for the other system. For example, after you configure the development system, you can export the configuration settings and import them into the production system, so you do not have to manually reconfigure the settings.

Settings that can be exported or imported:

- **Initial Data:** This data consists of the entire system configuration data when it is first set up. It includes all values and flags that were initially set.
- **Connector:** This data includes connector information for all systems (SAP, non- SAP, LDAP, and so on) that were configured.
- **Roles:** This data includes all roles that were created and imported to the system.
Note: Role export does not export role attributes. Role attributes must exist in the system before roles can be imported.
- **Workflow Configuration:** This data includes all information from initiator, custom approver determinators, stage, path, approvers, and the like.
- **User Defaults:** This data includes all mappings, values, and attribute settings.
- **HR Triggers:** This data includes all actions, rules, field mappings, and associated values and flag settings.

77) Which of the following statement is true regarding Enterprise Role Management?

Note: There is more than one correct answer to the question

   a. Provides automatic SAP Role Generation
   b. Role Naming standardization
   c. Provides change history for auditing and compliance
   d. Enforces consistency

Answer: a, b, c, d

Explanation:

Enterprise Role Management Enterprise Role Management simplifies the enterprise role engineering process:
• Provides a single enterprise role repository for role design, testing, and maintenance to enforce consistency and standardization

- Facilitates the role design process with a predefined (yet customizable) design methodology and workflow
- Supports the definition and documentation of role information, authorizations, and testing results
- Enforces the segregation-of-duties analysis during role design to prevent risks from entering application systems
- Provides change history for auditing and compliance
- Provides workflow approval for control checking and evaluation during role design
- Provides automatic SAP role generation
- Organizations can configure and enforce multiple role design processes within the company for different business purposes
- Companies can define multiple processes for different purposes, such as single role design process for all single roles
- Provides a central documentation repository for enterprise roles residing in SAP and non-SAP systems
- Naming convention to enforce role-naming standardization
- Enforces consistency, standardization, and ease of use for Enterprise Role Management

78) Which of the following are the examples of business process?

   Note: There is more than one correct answer to the question
   a. Finance
   b. Account Payables
   c. Procure to Pay
   d. Process Accumulation

Answer: a, b, c

Examples:

Business Processes A business process is a collection of related activities that produces something of value for your organization or business and is categorized based on your enterprise's organizational structure. A business process can be managerial, operational, or supporting, and can be defined narrowly or broadly, depending on your business needs.

When you create a role in Enterprise Role Management, the business process you assign to the role is one of the role's defining attributes and determines which sub processes you can assign to the role.

Examples of business processes are:

- Finance
- Accounts Payable
- Procure to Pay

Hint: Keep it simple. A sophisticated business process model might be a proper approach for process re-engineering, but the better approach for SAP Business Objects Access Control is to reduce complexity.

79) Suppose a company defines procurement as a business process then which of the following would be a sub process?

a. Purchasing
b. Promotion
c. Restriction
d. None of the above

Answer: a

Explanation:

Sub processes a sub process is a collection of related activities that produces something of value for your organization or business and is categorized based on your enterprise's organizational structure. It is a part of the business process. For example, if a company defines Procurement as a business process, then Purchasing would be a sub process.
A business process typically contains one or more sub processes. Each sub process must be linked to a business process

80) Which of the following Role attribute can be used to add attribute to a role that are specific to your company or Organization?

a. Business Process
b. Business Sub Processes
c. Custom Fields
d. Project/Release

Answer: c

Explanation:

Custom Fields Custom fields allow you to add attributes to a role that are specific to your company or organization. For instance, if you have a role that needs to be distinguished by region, adding a custom attribute allows you to assign a specific region when you create your role.

81) Which of the following is a prerequisite for creation of organization value mapping feature?

a. Background job must run
b. User assignment should be done
c. Role creation and assignment is mandatory
d. RFC connection to ERP system must be set

Answer: a

Explanation:

Organizational Value Mapping

If you want to restrict user access by organizational area, you can use the organizational value mapping feature to map roles to different organizational levels. To define all associated organizational values, you can create an organizational value map for each organizational area (such as North America, Europe, or Asia Pacific).

Prior to creating an organizational value map, you must run a background job to import existing organizational fields and values from your SAP ERP system. After the initial import, you can create a background job to schedule periodic synchronization to keep the data updated.

You always create an organizational value map with a primary organizational level and value, because Enterprise Role Management uses that to store and search for the organizational value. You can create multiple maps for the same primary organizational level and value combination. After the primary organizational level and value are set, you can define the values for all child organizational levels to complete the organizational value map. After you create the organizational value map, it can be used by all users as a basis to derive any master role.

82) With which of the following transaction Enterprise Role management in SAP Business Object is integrated?

   a. SU01
   b. SU24
   c. PFCG
   d. Both a&b

Answer: c

Explanation:

Authorization Data The second step in the role creation methodology is the authorization data. You can select the transactions that you want inside this role, and assign the authorizations to them. Enterprise Role Management uses the SU24 data that was synced with the back-end system to suggest the authorizations

Authorization Data with PFCG Integration Enterprise Role Management in SAP Business Objects Access Control is now integrated with transaction PFCG, the profile generator, in SAP ERP back-end systems of in SAP R/3 4.6C and higher. This allows you to leverage the advanced maintenance features in PFCG and allows security administrators to work in a familiar environment while maintenance is synchronized in Enterprise Role Management.

83) Suppose you would like to derive the multiple organization levels without having to use organizational map then which of the following feature is useful?

   a. Role creation
   b. Role Derivation
   c. Risk analysis on a Role
   d. Both a & b

Answer: b

Explanation:

Role Derivation With SAP Business Objects Access Control Enterprise Role Management, you can now derive a role during the role creation process by selecting the organizational level and inputting the organizational level value. You can push the role to all available organizational levels which exist in transactions in the master role you are deriving. This new feature gives you the ability to derive to multiple organizational levels during the role creation process without having to use the organizational map.

84) Which of the following web service can be used for workflow type creating and modifying mitigation control?

   a. /VirsaCCWFExitService5_2Service/Config1? wsdl&=document
   b. /VirsaCCWFExitService5_2Service/Config1?wsdl ^=document
   c. /AEWFExitServiceWS_5_2/Config1?wsdl&=document
   d. /VirsaCCWFExitService5_2Service/Config1?wsdl&=document

Answer: a

Explanation:

In Compliant User Provisioning, you can configure several workflow scenarios with the available SAP Business Objects Access Control Web Services. For example, you can set up the following workflow types within Compliant User Provisioning:

• For workflow type for creating and modifying mitigation control, you can use the following Web Service: /VirsaCCWFExitService5_2Service/Config1? wsdl&=document
• For workflow type for creating/modifying mitigation control assignment:
    /VirsaCCWFExitService5_2Service/Config1?wsdl&=document
• For Enterprise Role Management, you can configure the following Web Service:
    /AEWFExitServiceWS_5_2/Config1?wsdl&=document

- This is a workflow type for creating and modifying risks:
    /VirsaCCWFExitService5_2Service/Config1?wsdl&=document
- You can configure a SoD Review workflow: AEWFExitServiceWS_ 5_2/Config1?wsdl&=document

85) Which of the following web services can be configured in Enterprise Role Management?

Note: There is more than one correct answer to the question

  a. Risk Analysis
  b. Transaction Usage
  c. Mitigation Control
  d. Functions

Answer: a, b, c, d

Explanation:

Enterprise Role Management When configuring Web Services for Enterprise Role Management, you will also need to navigate through the *SAP Net Weaver Administration* page and go to *Web Services Navigation*. Within Enterprise Role Management, you can configure the following Web services:

- Web Services Info. for CC Risk Analysis
- Web Services Info. for CC Transaction Usage
- Web Services Info. for CC Mitigation Control
- Web Services Info. for CC Functions
- Web Services Info. for AE Workflow

An ID and password are required when configuring these Web Services. When assigning an ID, make sure that the user ID has the SAP Business Objects Access Control roles assigned so that the user is able to access each of the areas listed above.

86) Which of the following options are available for security reports?

Note: There is more than one correct answer to the question

  a. Users by ID
  b. By Org Level
  c. Authorization count
  d. Expiry roles of users

Audit Reports

You can view action reports within audit reports. These action reports can be used to identify the rules in Risk Analysis and Remediation.

Security Reports The following options are available for security reports:

- Users by User ID
- User Authorization Count
- List Expired and Expiring Roles for Users
- Users by Organizational level

87) Which of the following report allows us to review user access?

   a. SoD Review History Report
   b. User access Review History Report
   c. User/Role History Report
   d. Both a & b

Answer: b
Explanation:

Compliant User Provisioning

A variety of Compliant User Provisioning reports are located under the *Informer* tab. Two very important reports are the SoD Review History report and the User Access Review History report.

- SoD Review History report: This report can assist you in determining the SoDs that have been remediated through the workflow process.

- User Access Review History Report: This report allows you to review user accesses

88) Which of the following report allows us to view the changes made to the role through Enterprise Role Management?

   a. SoD Review History Report
   b. ERM Change History
   c. PFCG Change history
   d. User access Review Change History

Answer: b

Explanation:

Enterprise Role Management There are several Enterprise Role Management reports available under the *Informer* tab, but there are some critical reports under the *Role Management* tab, which allow you to view the change history within ERM or PFCG.

• Enterprise Role Management Change History: This report allows you to view the changes made to roles through Enterprise Role Management.
• PFCG Change History: This report allows you to view changes made to roles through PFCG.

By viewing both of these reports, you can view the history of changes to roles that occurred through ERM or through PFCG. You can determine discrepancies by comparing roles and their transaction codes.

89) Which of the following solution will contribute to enhanced performance and helps to identify the risks?

   a. SAP GRC 10.0
   b. SoD Reports
   c. SAP Enterprise Portal
   d. SAP Solution

Answer: a

Explanation:

SAP Business Objects Governance, Risk, and Compliance (GRC) can help to document and manage the prevention and/or detection of the identified risks and also document and manage the mitigation or remediation of the identified risks or issues. This solution can also serve as an audit trail during period end review processes.

Companies with advanced perspectives of risk and mature risk management practices recognize that risk is present throughout their business.

Risk comes in many flavors:
- Strategic risk
- Operational risk
- Financial risk
- Fraud risk
- Compliance risk
- Reputational risk
- Supply chain risk

90) GRC's continuous transaction monitoring allows you to which of the following three key benefits?

    a. Quality Improvement
    b. Increase margin Contribution
    c. Increase insight into business activities
    d. All of the above

Answer: d

Explanation:

GRC's continuous transaction monitoring solution allows you to identify and correct errors, waste, abuse, policy violations, and potential fraud. These issues can only be revealed through in-depth analysis of transactions that are recorded as business activities are completed. This in-depth analysis allow you to achieve three key benefits:

1. Improve the quality and speed of your business processes
2. Increase insight into business activities
3. Increase margin contribution

GRC Integration

91) Which of the following integrations are applicable across the GRC 10.0 Solution?

Note: There is more than one correct answer to the question

a. Access Control Integration
b. Risk Management Integration
c. Process Control Integration
d. Solution Integration

Answer: a, b, c

Explanation:

The following integrations are applicable across the GRC 10.0 solution:
- Crystal reports
- Document Search via TREX
- Business Intelligence (BI)
- Business Warehouse (BW)
- Other SAP Systems
- Non-SAP Systems
- LDAP Integration

Access Control Integrations
- HR Triggers
- Identity Management
- Process Control and Risk Management Shared Master Data Integration Points

Risk Management Integrations
- SAP Project System
- SAP Plant Maintenance
- SAP Environmental Health & Safety
- SAP Issue Management
- SAP Policy Management

Process Control Integrations
- Process Integration
- SoD Integration

92) Which of the following functionality allows the creation of automatic access risks?

a. Identity Management
b. Process control Management
c. HR Triggers
d. Both a & b

Answer: c

Explanation:

Access Control Integration: HR Triggers The HR Triggers functionality of Access Control 10.0 allows the creation of automatic access requests, corresponding to changes in master data in SAP or Non-SAP HR systems. When an event is triggered in the SAP HR system, such as hiring a new employee, rules are applied and a corresponding action to create a workflow request is initiated in Access Control. The request can be processed through workflow and can be provisioned to the back-end system by direct assignment or indirect assignment.

The configuration of HR Triggers in Access Control 10.0 includes the configuration of actions, rules, and field mapping.

Note: Users do not need to complete an access request form.

93) Which of the following Scenarios with IdM Integration are supported?

Note: There is more than one correct answer to the question

a. GRC driven provisioning
b. Access provisioning
c. Solution provisioning
d. IdM Driven provisioning

Answer: a, d

Explanation:

GRC Access Control provides robust integration with IdM solutions and continues to focus on its core competencies of risk, SoD and remediation. To support this strategy, Access Control integrates with market leading IdM vendors like SUN, Novell and integrate and optimize for SAP Net Weaver IdM.

User Provisioning Scenarios with IdM Integration

Two scenarios are supported:

GRC-driven provisioning
IdM-driven provisioning.

GRC-driven provisioning is initiated in GRC, provisioned by GRC for SAP systems, and provisioned in IdM for non-SAP systems. IdM-driven provisioning is initiated in IdM, submitted to GRC through Web Services, provisioned by GRC for SAP systems, and provisioned in IdM for non-SAP systems.

User Assignments

When integrating with IdM solutions, there are 2 possible scenarios available:
- Access Control Driven Provisioning
    - Request created in AC
    - Risk Analysis and Approval completed in AC
    - SAP content is provisioned from AC
    - Non-SAP provisioning information sent to IdM for provisioning
- IdM-Driven Provisioning
    - Request created in IdM
    - Request information is sent to AC for Risk Analysis and Approval
    - SAP content is provisioned from AC
    - Non-SAP provisioning information sent to IdM for provisioning

94) Integration for Process control 10.0 includes which of the following?

   a. Process Integration
   b. SoD Integration
   c. Access Integration
   d. Risk Integration

Answer: a, b

Explanation:

Integrations for Process Control 10.0 include:
- Process Integration
- SoD Integration

Process Integration allows you to monitor deficiencies in other systems. The Process Integration Proxy must be completed before you can proceed on the portal.

The Process Integration proxy is used to monitor another system, so only Outbound proxy is supported.

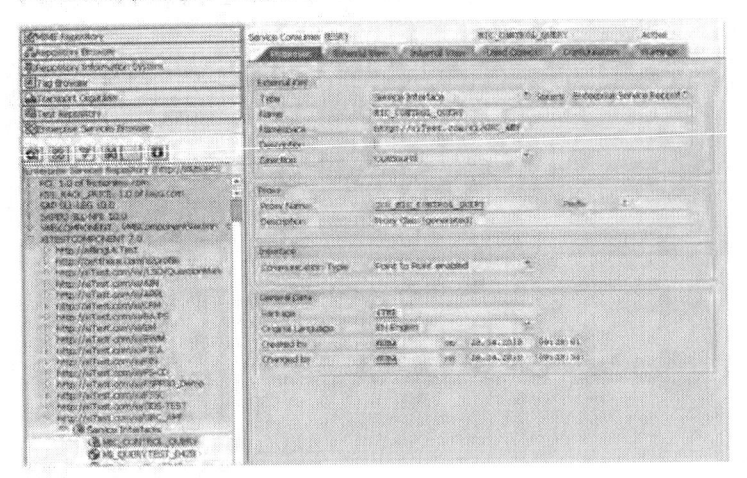

95) Which of the following integrations of Risk Management 10.0 include?

Note: There is more than one correct answer to the question

   a. SAP Project system
   b. SAP Plant Maintenance
   c. SAP Environment Health & Safety
   d. SAP Issue Management
   e. SAP Policy Management

Answer: a, b, c, d, e

Explanation:

Risk Management Integration Risk Management integrates with several other systems to help users identify and manage risk from one location.

Integrations for Risk Management 10.0 include:
- SAP Project System
- SAP Plant Maintenance
- SAP Environmental Health & Safety
- SAP Issue Management
- SAP Policy Management

96) Which of the following statements are true regarding SAP Project system?

Note: There is more than one correct answer to the question

a. It allows you to trigger automatic creation of Project
b. It allows you to track the status of project definition
c. It is maintained by project manager
d. Current status is obtained by a periodic background job

Answer: a, b, c, d

Explanation:

Risk Management - SAP Project System Integration Project System Integration allows you to:

• Trigger automatic creation of project definition in Project Systems from Risk Management
• Track the status of the project definition from the remote Project Systems system

A Risk Manager is not required to have any Project System background to create a project out of a Risk Management response. The project is actually maintained by a Project Manager or another responsible person and Risk Managers may only track the current status of the project they created. Current status is obtained by a periodic background job. The Risk Manager just opens the response.

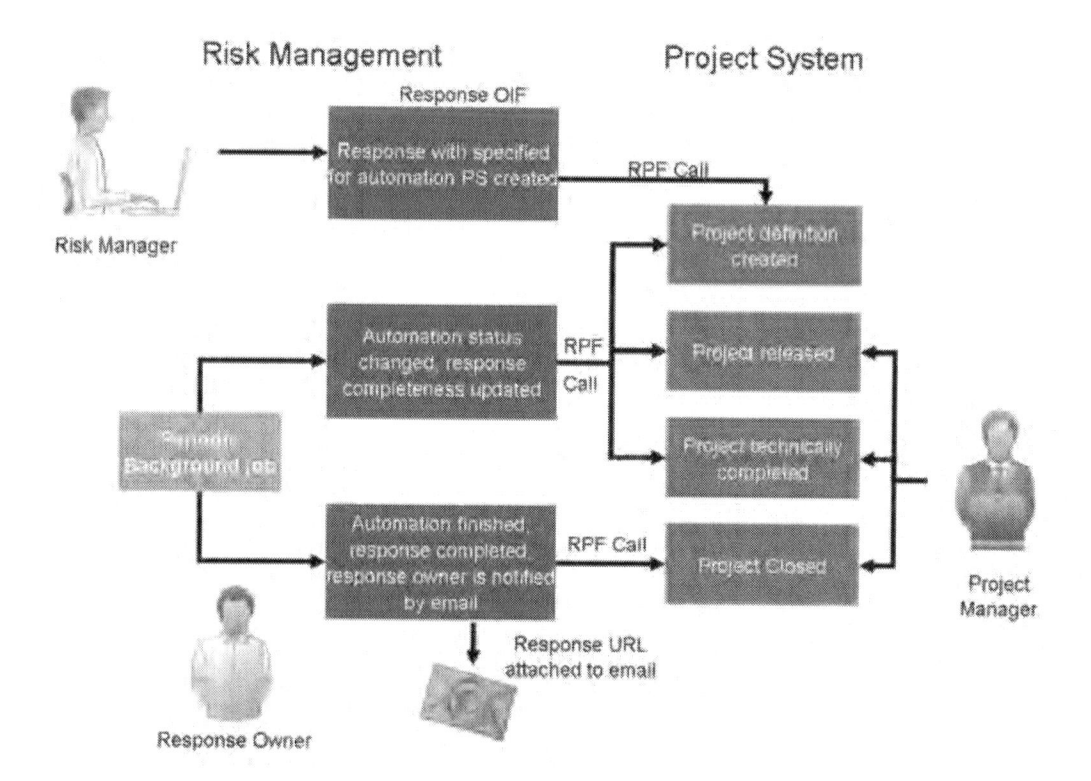

97) Integration between Risk Management and Plant Maintenance allows you to which of the following?

Note: There is more than one correct answer to the question

   a. Invokes automatic creation of notification
   b. Tracking status of notification
   c. No automatic generation
   d. None of the above

Answer: a, b

Explanation:

Plant Maintenance Integration Some responses for risks require that service, maintenance, or quality inspection procedures be performed over the technical objects or fixed assets. Therefore, automatic creation of Plant Maintenance notifications directly from Risk Management can be helpful in this regard.

The integration between Risk Management and Plant Maintenance allows you to:
- Invoke automatic creation of notification in Plant Maintenance from Risk Management
- Track the status of the notification from the remote Plant Maintenance system

Response Automation Benefits
- Automatic creation of Plant Maintenance notifications directly from Risk Management help with risk responses that require service, maintenance, or quality inspection procedures be performed over the technical objects or fixed assets

The Risk manager is not required to have any Plant Maintenance background to create a notification out of a Risk Management response. A notification is actually processed by a Plant Maintenance manager or another responsible person and Risk manager may only track the current status of the notification created. Current status is obtained by a periodic background job. To see this, the Risk manager just opens the response

98) Which of the following are the features of Issue Management Integration?

Note: There is more than one correct answer to the question

   a. Supports central categorization
   b. Supports management of Issues
   c. Provides enterprise wide visibility of issues

d. Allows flexible determination

Answer: a, b, c, d

Explanation:

Risk Management - Issue Management Integration Issue Management allows the management of issues identified outside of the standard testing and assessment process.

Features include:
• Enables reporting process for risk and compliance related issues outside of standard evaluation processes
• Supports central categorization and management of issues
• Allows flexible determination of appropriate responses/remediation procedures
• Provides enterprise-wide visibility of issues and their remediation statuses

Note: Ad Hoc issues can be created during the Aggregation of Deficiencies and Sign-Off level, but currently are not considered. If you create an issue while working these tasks, you do not get an error message.

The integration between Risk Management and Issue Management allows you to:
- Assign issues to the Risk Management objects
- Update response completeness based on closing the issue

Integration Benefits Include:
- Enhances the Process Control solution to provide extended capability and transparency to external auditing process
- Improves the flexibility and traceability on enterprise-wide compliance issue management across all GRC applications
- Ad Hoc Issue functionality helps users to document their complete compliance effort in one tool, rather than documenting external issues in a different tool

99) How can you begin to leverage your Governance, Risk and Compliance programs to optimize the performance?

Note: There is more than one correct answer to the question

a. Know your business
b. Know Business related risks
c. Know compliance and Policy Requirements
d. Know what reserves your company has for litigation

Answer: a, b, c

Explanation:

Knowledge of your business, related risks, and compliance and policy requirements are the starting point to leveraging your Governance, Risk, and Compliance programs to optimize performance.

100) **SAP Business Objects GRC solutions are comprised of three main areas of capabilities?**

Note: There is more than one correct answer to the question

a. Avoid
b. Analyze
c. Monitor
d. Manage

Answer: b, c, d

Explanation:

Analyze, Manage, and Monitor are the three main areas of capabilities
SAP Business Objects GRC solutions help companies to proactively balance risk and opportunity through three main concepts:

- Customers can better manage risk, compliance, and other GRC initiatives
- Customers can better protect their value
- Organizations can perform better.

Ultimately, the goal is to enable organizations to see all risks and compliance issues so that they can make optimal decisions in light of both the opportunity ahead and the related risks.

101) **Which component in the SAP Business Objects GRC solution supports Compliance Management by providing documentation of compliance structures and related compliance initiatives?**

a. Risk Management
b. Access Control
c. Process Control
d. Global Trade Services

Answer: c

Explanation:

Process Control – document, monitor and review processes; document and monitor issue remediation of issues

102) **Which component in the SAP Business Objects GRC solution provides the ability to manage and monitor user privileges?**

   a. Risk Management
   b. Access Control
   c. Process Control
   d. Global Trade Services

Answer: b

Explanation:

SAP Business Objects Access Control addresses these challenges by enabling businesses to confidently manage and reduce access risk across the enterprise. It helps to prevent unauthorized access – including segregation of duties (SoD) and critical access – and achieve real-time visibility to access risk, minimizing the time and cost of access risk management.

The Access Control solution unifies access risk analysis and remediation, business role management, compliant identity management, emergency privilege management, and provides a holistic, enterprise-wide view in real time. It can help ensure day-to-day compliance, provide comprehensive management oversight, and perform effective and complete audits. The result is an improved ability to protect information and prevent fraud while minimizing the time and cost of access risk management.

103) **The Configurable User Interface allows configuration to determine?**

   a. Field status by application components
   b. Field status by regulation
   c. A and B
   d. None of the above; programming is required

Answer: c

Explanation:

The Configurable User Interface allows configuration to determine field status by application components and by regulation.

Configurable User Interface allows configuration to determine field status by application components. For example, the organization field "Average Cost per Control" can be shown for those users authorized for Process Control and hidden for those users authorized for Access Control. Field statuses (required field, optional field, displayed, or hidden) can be selected by field by component or even regulation, if applicable. Changes to the field status are reflected in the user interface without requiring programming.

104) Considering the business use and purpose of the Access Control solution, which of the following would be logical integrations?

Note: There is more than one correct answer to the question

   a. HR Triggers
   b. SAP Issue Management
   c. Identity Management
   d. SAP Crystal Reports

Answer: a, c, d

Explanation:

HR Triggers, Identity Management, and SAP Crystal Reports are all logical integrations with the Access Control solution.

The Access Control solution unifies access risk analysis and remediation, business role management, compliant identity management, emergency privilege management, and provides a holistic, enterprise-wide view in real time. It can help ensure day-to-day compliance, provide comprehensive management oversight, and perform effective and complete audits. The result is an improved ability to protect information and prevent fraud while minimizing the time and cost of access risk management.

Information Architecture

105) What are the goals of Information architecture harmonization include?

Note: There is more than one correct answer to the question

- a. Consistent user experience
- b. Optimization
- c. Enhance
- d. None of the above

Answer: a, b, c

Explanation:

Harmonization Goals of the Information Architecture

Goals of information architecture harmonization include:
• Providing a consistent user experience across GRC

- Optimizing for users of multiple GRC applications by minimizing redundancy and streamlining navigation.
- Enhancing the user experience while providing users the tools needed to do their job.

106) A key feature of the GRC 10.0 information architecture is?

    a. Separate work inboxes for each solution component
    b. A single shared work inbox for all solution components
    c. A single shared work inbox for Process Control and Risk Management
    d. A single shared work inbox for Process Control and Access Control

Answer: b

Explanation:

The GRC 10.0 Information Architecture:
- Provides direct navigation to Access Control, Process Control and Risk Management components.
- Eliminates redundant menu items.
- Varies based upon user authorization.
- Allows configuration changes for the SAP Net Weaver Portal component or SAP Net Weaver Business Client software.

107) Which of the following determines the presentation of user interface elements?

    a. Information Architecture
    b. GRC Control process
    c. GRC Access Process
    d. GRC User Access

Answer: a

Explanation:

The information architecture (IA) determines the presentation of user interface elements:

- Menu structure
- Tabs
- Navigation alternatives

The IA presents the application or solution to its users and defines much of the initial user experience.

108) Which of the following statements are true, to access GRC 10.0 solutions, you must have at least the following?

Note: There is more than one correct answer to the question

a. Portal Authorization
b. NWBC Authorization
c. Applicable PFCG Base roles
d. PFCG role relative to specific component

Answer: a, b, c, d

Explanation:

To access GRC 10.0 solutions, you must have at least the following:
- Portal authorization or NWBC authorization
- Applicable PFCG base roles
- PFCG role(s) relative to specific components (AC, PC, RM) to be used

To configure the IMG, you need:
- PFCG role(s) relative to specific components to be configured
- PFCG role(s) sufficient to configure SAP workflow and other non-GRC technologies
- PFCG role(s) on GRC and non-GRC systems to set up continuous monitoring

PFCG refers to the SAP NetWeaver transaction that deals with role maintenance and profile generation

109) If you use Access Control 10.0 with other GRC solution components, you can leverage this functionality to?

a. Create GRC users
b. Assign and manage PFCG roles used with GRC
c. Perform SoD analysis for PFCG role authorizations
d. Perform SoD analysis for entity-level authorization

Answer: a, b, c

Explanation:

SAP BusinessObjects Access Control 10.0

If you use Access Control 10.0 with other GRC solutions, you can leverage this functionality to:
- Manage PFCG roles used with GRC
- Create GRC users
- Assign GRC PFCG roles to users
- Perform SOD analysis for PFCG role authorizations

Assignment of these authorizations, however, must be done in the respective component:
- Assignment of entity-level authorization (via application role assignment)
- Assignment of ticket-based authorization (via substitution or transfer)

110) Which of the following determine what users see in the GRC 10.0 user interface?

Note: There is more than one correct answer to the question

   a. Product Licensing
   b. User Interface Framework Configuration
   c. Roles and Authorizations
   d. Work Centers

Answer: a, b, c

Explanation:

Product licensing, the user interface framework configuration, and roles & authorizations determine what users see in the GRC 10.0 user interface.

The end user sees is determined by a combination of factors, as

- The product licensing determines access to components
- The UI framework configuration controls what fields are displayed to each underlying component
- Roles/authorizations determine more granular access, all the way down to individual business entities (such as Control XYZ in Organization ABC) in the case of Process Control and Risk Management

111) Which of the following statements are true regarding work center in SAP Net weaver Portal component?

Note: There is more than one correct answer to the question

   a. Work centers are defined in PCD roles for portal
   b. Work centers are defined in PFCG for NWBC

c. Location of application folders are controlled by SAP Net Weaver Launch pad Application
   d. Service map is generated dynamically

Answer: a, b, c, d

Explanation:

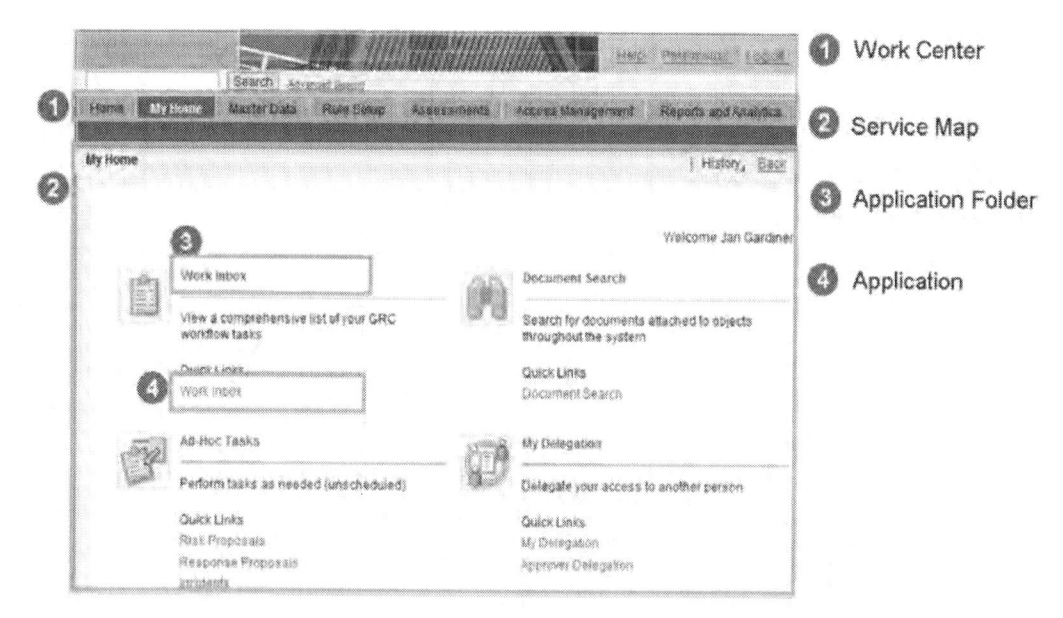

The above shows the My Homework center as displayed in the SAP Net Weaver Portal component. The look would be similar, but not identical, in the SAP Net Weaver Business Client (NWBC) software.

1. Work centers are defined in PCD roles for the Portal and in PFCG roles for NWBC. The work centers are fixed in each base role. SAP delivers these roles, but they can be modified by the customer.

2. The locations of application folders and subordinate applications within the service map are controlled by the SAP Net Weaver Launchpad application. You may see this in the IMG configuration.

3. The service map is then generated dynamically based upon user authorization. That is, if the user does not have authorization to see given application folders or applications, they will be hidden from view (not grayed out).

Work Centers

112) **Which of the following statement are true regarding Work centers?**

Note: There is more than one correct answer to the question

   a. Provide a central access point for GRC 10.0
   b. Are independent of customer licensing

c. Can be customized by a system administrator
d. Do not contained shared tasks across solution components

Answer: a, c

Explanation:

Work centers provide a central access point for GRC 10.0 and can be customized by a system administrator.
Work centers provide a central access point for GRC 10.0. They can be organized based on what the customer has been licensed to operate. Delivered work centers are shown below.

The default delivered system contains the work centers displayed above. However, your system administrator can customize the work centers to support your organization's preferred structures. Depending on the products that you have licensed, different components of the GRC solution are displayed (Access Control, Process Control, or Risk Management).

113) My Homework center allows you to the following?

Note: There is more than one correct answer to the question

a. Acts as central point for all other work centers
b. View, access and perform all work flow tasks
c. Delegates the tasks
d. View and process the data

Answer: b, c, d

Explanation:

My Home Work Center
The My Homework center allows you to:
• View, access, and perform workflow tasks assigned to you, including viewing completed reports that you scheduled.

- Perform document searches across all documents (including document content) for which you have authorization.
- Assign delegates to perform your tasks or activities.
- View and process your user data.

The service maps and applications under each work center are controlled by your access. If you are a delegate and choose to work as that person, you will inherit their authorization.

114) Which of the following work centers is only used in Access Control?

   a. Rule Setup
   b. Master Data
   c. Assessments
   d. Setup

Answer: d

Explanation:

Setup Work Center for Access Control The Setup work center is available in Access Control and provides links to the following areas:
Access Rule Maintenance
Exception Access Rules
Critical Access Rules
Generated Rules
Organizations
Mitigating Controls
Super user Assignment
Super user Maintenance
Access Owners

The Access Rule Maintenance section allows you to manage access rule sets, functions, and the access risks used to identify access violations Under Exception Access Rules, you can manage rules that supplement access rules. The Critical Access Rules section allows you to define additional rules that identify access to critical roles and profiles.

115) Which of the following Rules section allows you to identify individual roles and profiles that pose an access risk to your company?

   a. Access Rule Maintenance
   b. Critical Access Rule
   c. Exception access rule
   d. Generated Rule

Answer: b

Explanation:

The Access Rule Maintenance section includes the ability to maintain rule sets, access risks and functions.
The Critical Access Rules section allows you to identify individual roles and profiles that pose an access risk to your company. If your system uses profiles, you may have defined profiles that pose an access risk. Make sure that you designate these profiles as critical profiles.
The Exception Access Rules section allows you to eliminate false positives based on organizational-level restrictions. This functionality was created to aid exception-based reporting for organizational rules and supplemental rules.
The Generated Rules section shows generated rules and related details including access risks, functions.

116) Which of the following sections contains Assessment work center?

   Note: There is more than one correct answer to the question

   a. Surveys
   b. Manual Test Plans
   c. Incident Management
   d. Reports

Answer: a, b, c, d

Explanation:

Assessments Work Center
Depending on the GRC products you have licensed, the Assessments work center contains the following sections:
Surveys
Manual Test Plans
Risk Assessments
Incident Management
Scenario Management
Assessment Planning
Reports

117) Which of the following work center section allows you to create a manual test plans?

a. Surveys Section
b. Manual Test Plan
c. Risk Assessment
d. Incident Management

Answer: b

Explanation:

The Surveys section of the Assessments work center provides setup of survey components. Within GRC, surveys are used to obtain information on the existence and evaluation of risks (Risk Management) or the adequacy of controls (Process Control). Surveys are used to carry out assessments of objects such as risks, activities, controls and policies, for example.

The Manual Test Plans section allows you to create a manual test plans which consist of test steps performed to determine whether a control is operating effectively.
The Risk Assessments section enables you to create activities to be evaluated for risks and opportunities, such as projects or business processes.
The Incident Management section provides documentation of risks that occur—that is, incidents.

118) Which of the following statements are true regarding Adhoc issues?

Note: There is more than one correct answer to the question

a. Identify and manages issues
b. Associate the issues
c. Enables mass import
d. Manages check in

Answer: a, b

Explanation:

Policy Management:
Manage policy lifecycle: creating, maintaining, reviewing, approving, updating
Assign policy scope to organizations, business processes, activities, users/roles
Distribute and manage policy acknowledgement, quizzes and surveys
Report policy status and compliance

Ad Hoc Issues:
Identify, remediate and manage issues not associated with compliance evaluations
Associate issues with a variety of business entities such as organizations, risks, regulations, controls

Content Lifecycle Management:
Enable mass import, export and edit of master data content
Manage check-in, version control and deployment of content
Support third-party content deployment with comparison to existing customer content

119) Which of the following feature is designed as end to end process begins with creating and approving policies?

   a. Policy Management
   b. Ad Hoc issue
   c. Content Lifecycle
   d. Both a & b

Answer: a

Explanation:

Policy Management is a common function available to those companies licensing SAP Business Objects Process Control 10.0 or SAP Business Objects Risk Management 10.0.

The end-to-end process begins with creating and approving policies, which often involves attaching or linking the policy documents. You indicate the scope of each policy by assigning it to organizations, processes or activities, and people. You also may associate controls or ERM risks to the policy.

Thereafter, you distribute the policy to those affected by it and, if desired, you may require formal acceptance or acknowledgment. In addition, you may require that survey assessments or quizzes be completed to indicate understanding of the policy. Information on acceptance, assessments or quizzes can be reported to demonstrate the level of compliance. For the reason that policies may be widely distributed throughout an organization, an SAP logon is not required to receive the policy or to acknowledge it.

120) Ad hoc issues management is a common function available to those companies licensing?

   Note: There is more than one correct answer to the question

a. Access Control
b. Risk Management
c. Process Control
d. Access Control and Process Control
e. Process Control and Risk Management
f. Risk Management and Access Control

Answer: b, c, e

Explanation:

Ad hoc issues management is a common function available to those companies licensing Process Control, Risk Management, or both. Ad hoc issues management is a common function available to those companies licensing SAP Business Objects Process Control 10.0 or SAP Business Objects Risk Management 10.0.

This feature is designed to enable identification, remediation and tracking of issues not associated with scheduled compliance evaluations. Examples of ad hoc issues include external audit findings, issues discovered by inspections, and problems reported by individuals outside formal compliance processes. If an issue is not fully complete, it is routed via workflow to an issue administrator, who reviews, completes and assigns the issue. Thereafter, the issue is similar to an evaluation-based issue reported in PC—that is, it may be remediated and then closed. You may associate issues with a variety of business entities such as organizations, risks, regulations, and controls. You may also assign a source of the issue; the sources available are configurable in the IMG.

121) Which of the following function allows external content to be packaged and imported to CLM repository?

a. Policy Management
b. Ad Hoc issue
c. Content Lifecycle
d. Both a & b

Answer: c

Explanation:

SAP BusinessObjects Access Control 10.0

The Content Lifecycle Management (CLM) function allows external content to be packaged and imported to the CLM repository. This external content could be company data imported for the first time into the GRC solution during implementation, or it could be content developed by third parties. Once imported to CLM, you can review the content, decide what to deploy, and resolve any content conflicts (if the content has been previously deployed). Deploy the content you select, then manage it as needed in GRC (currently RM and PC components). As needed, you may checkpoint and export the content managed in GRC and import it again to the CLM repository. This is done so that it can be edited on a mass basis or used to compare your current content with updated external content you receive.

122) User interface configuration framework enables the following?

   a. Reduce Redundancy
   b. Configuring different views
   c. Using common and centralized data
   d. All of the above

Answer: d

Explanation:

The User Interface Configuration Framework enables:
- Using a single UI launch point for maintaining shared GRC master data across applications and compliance initiatives (regulations), if applicable
- Configuring different views for different users of the same master data entity by application component and regulation
- Using common and centralized master data to reduce redundancy while supporting entity attributes that can be specific to regulations

123) Following steps can be performed to configure the user interface status at the field level?

   Note: There is more than one correct answer to the question

   a. Regulation specific configuration
   b. Local Change configuration
   c. Field status Configuration by Application component
   d. Filed status configuration by Regulation

Answer: a, b, c, d

Explanation:

To configure the user interface status at the field level, you can perform the following steps:
- Regulation-Specific Configuration: You can specify whether or not a field has regulation-specific values.
- Allow Local Change Configuration: You can specify whether or not a field can be changed locally (provided that sub process is assigned with "Allow Local Changes" enabled in PC).
- Field Status Configuration by Application Component: You can set the field status for individual application components as one of the following: Required, Optional, Display, or Hidden. (This is relevant to shared master data for AC and RM, as well as PC.)
- Field Status Configuration by Regulation: You can set the field status for an individual regulation. By default, all regulation-specific fields have the Optional status. The available field statuses are: Required, Optional, Display, or Hidden.

124) Which of the following statements are true regarding Regulation specific values?

Note: There is more than one correct answer to the question

a. Fields are maintained in table GRFNFLDRGSP
b. These are related to process control only
c. These are related to Access control only
d. These are related to User access control only

Answer: a, b

Explanation:

Regulation-Specific Values

SAP has already maintained a set of fields as Regulation-Specific Fields in control table GRFNFLDRGSP. You can change these settings in IMG → Governance, Risk and Compliance → Shared master data settings → Maintain Field-Based Configuration → Regulation-Specific Configuration.

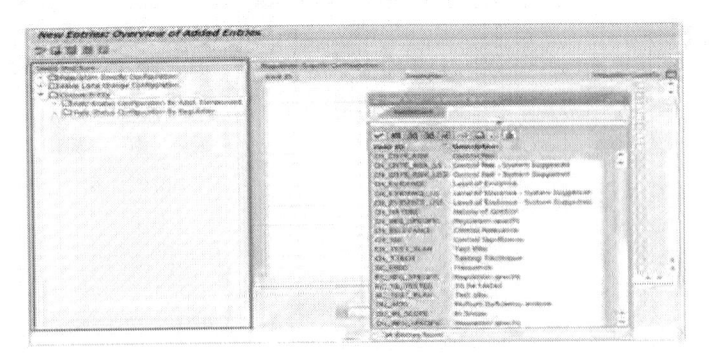

Only those fields that exist in control table GRFNFLDRGSP (also appear in the F4 help list) can be regulation-specific fields. Keep in mind that regulation-specific fields relate to Process Control only.

125) From which of the following control table fields can be set to allow local changes?

   a. GRFNFLDLCHG
   b. GRFNFLDRGSP
   c. GRFNFLDRAFG
   d. GRFNFLDRSYT

Answer: a

Explanation:

SAP has also maintained a set of fields as Local Changes Allowed Fields in control table GRFNFLDLCHG. You can change these settings in *IMG → Governance, Risk and Compliance → Shared Master Data Settings → Maintain Field-Based Configuration → Allow Local Change Configuration*.

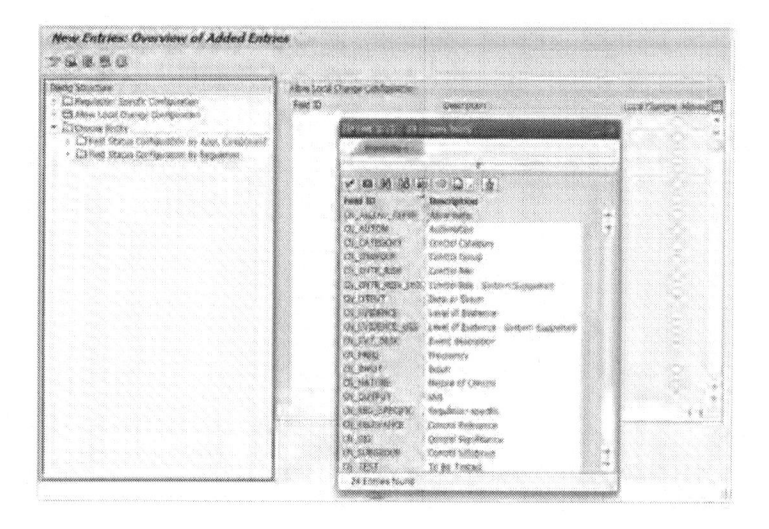

Only those fields exist in control table GRFNFLDLCHG (also appear in the F4 help list) can be set to allow local changes. Local Changes Allowed fields relate to PC only because these are dependent upon the method of assigning sub processes to organizations. That is, if during assignment of a sub process to an organization the sub process is set to not allow local changes (similar to assigning with reference in prior versions of PC), the settings here do not apply to that sub process for that organization nor to subordinate controls within that sub process.

126) Which of the following statement is not true regarding Field status configuration by Application component?

   a. SAP has defined set of fields as configurable fields in table GRFNFLD

b. Default UI field status is optional
c. It is recommended to make changes directly to table
d. Changes can be done through IMG directly

Answer: c

Explanation:

SAP has defined a set of fields as Configurable Fields in control table GRFNFLD. You can maintain the UI status for these fields for each entity for different Application Components in IMG → Governance, Risk and Compliance → Shared Master Data settings → Maintain Field-Based Configuration → Field Status Configuration by Appl. Component.

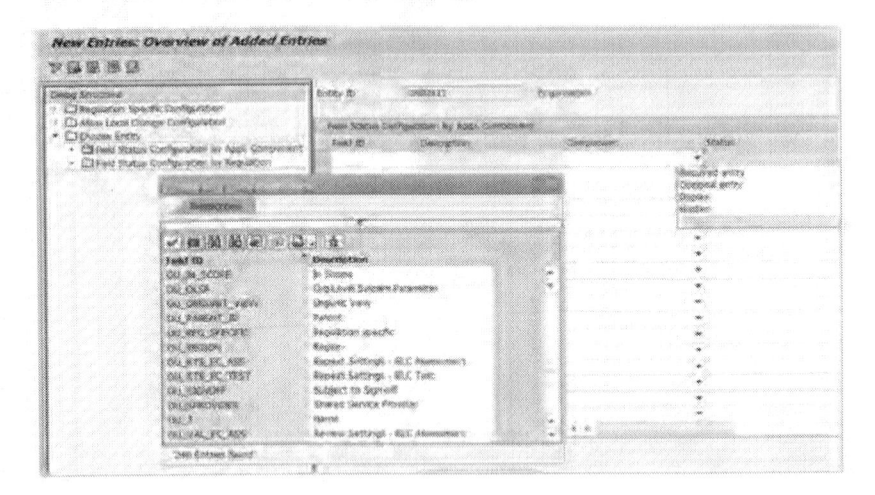

Users can only maintain the UI status for those fields that exist in control table GRFNFLD (also appears in the F4 help list for Field ID). The default UI field status is Optional.

The predefined Field UI Status Configuration by Application is maintained in the table GRFNAPPFLD. It is recommended that you do not make changes directly to the GRFNAPPFLD table, but instead use this IMG activity

127) **Shared master data involves the following?**

a. Manual synchronization of data
b. Decreased risk of inconsistent master data
c. Redundant maintenance
d. Required sharing of organizations

Answer: b

Explanation:

Shared master data involves decreased risk of inconsistent master data. Sharing of organizations is optional, but not required.

SAP Business Objects GRC 10.0 is an integrated solution with Risk Management, Process Control and Access Control being contained in a single SAP component. These solutions work together to product a more harmonized and complete picture of the GRC environment. Several configuration items and attributes are shared items between 2 or more of the components. These shared items now can be set up one time and consumed by any of the installed programs as needed rather than maintaining the same information in multiple spots. This reduces the amount of configuration and / or maintenance involved as well as the need to synchronize master data (whether manually or by system) between the components and therefore reduces the amount of time and the possibility of the data being out of sync with the other solutions within the GRC solution.

128) Master data-related implementation considerations for organizations include?

Note: There is more than one correct answer to the question

a. To what extent will companies share harmonized structures
b. To what extent does the company work in separate silos
c. Who is responsible for maintaining organization hierarchies
d. How does a company plan to evolve in the future

Answer: a, b, c, d

Explanation:

Master Data Related Implementation Considerations for Organizations

- What organization structures are used today for access, compliance and risk management?
- To what extent does the company work in separate silos today?
- If there is little or no sharing or harmonized structures, does the company hope to change that in the future?
- Who is responsible for maintaining organization hierarchies?

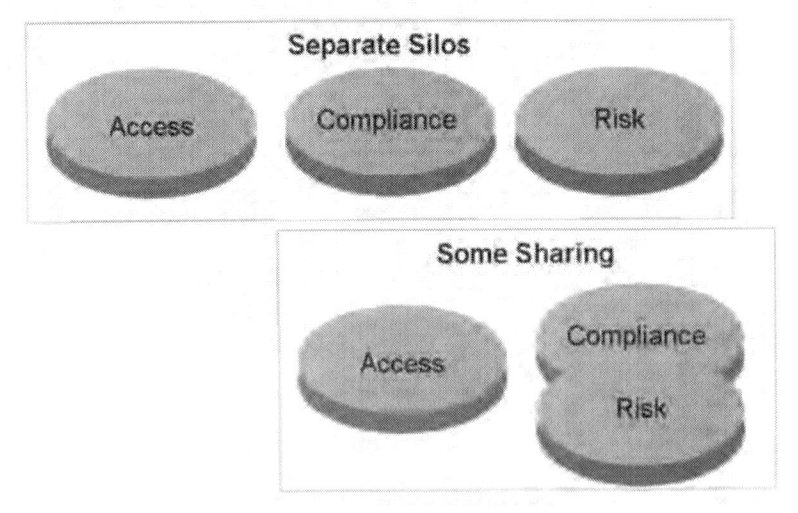

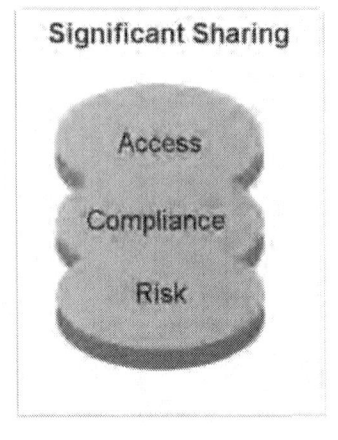

129) To access the IMG, first logon to ABAP client for GRC 10.0 then which of the following tcode needs to be executed?

    a. SRMG
    b. SPRO
    c. SDRO
    d. SCRO

Answer: b

Explanation:

In prior releases, configuration of Process Control and Risk Management were separate IMG activities with some overlap. Prior Access Control releases did not provide configuration using the IMG. To streamline configuration, the GRC 10.0 solutions' IMG identifies activities which are shared among multiple products

To access the IMG, first log into the ABAP client for GRC 10.0, then execute transaction SPRO. Click SAP Reference IMG to view the IMG nodes and customizing activities

130) From the IMG, you can configure the following?

    Note: There is more than one correct answer to the question

a. General settings for Access Control, Process Control, or Risk Management
b. Shared master data settings
c. Reporting
d. Common component settings for those solution components in use.

Answer: a, b, c, d

Explanation:

To access the IMG, first log into the ABAP client for GRC 10.0, then execute transaction SPRO. Click SAP Reference IMG to view the IMG nodes and customizing activities. From here, you can configure:

General settings as needed for Access Control, Process Control, or Risk Management
Shared master data settings
Reporting
Common component settings for those components in use

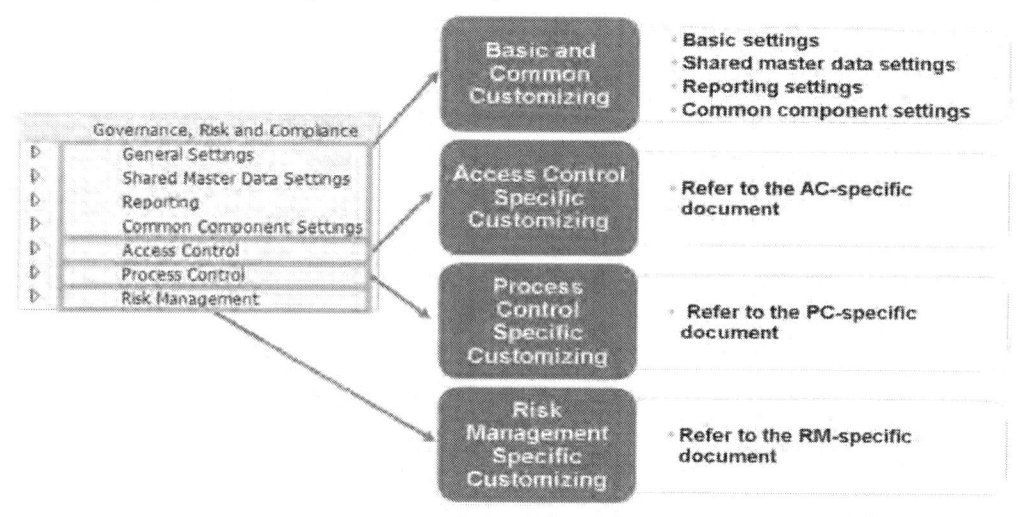

131) Which of the following are the prerequisites before beginning the Functional Implementation?

Note: There is more than one correct answer to the question

a. Complete technical setup
b. Complete RFC and background jobs config
c. Activating the BC sets
d. Obtaining the necessary authorization roles

Answer: a, c, d

Explanation:

Prerequisites before Beginning the Functional Implementation

1. Complete technical setup
2. Activate applicable BC sets based upon customer requirements
3. Obtain the authorization roles necessary for access to the IMG

Note: Only activate the timeframe-related BC sets if the customer is on a calendar year because January to December is delivered in the BC set. Some IMG activities are only needed if you would like to change the delivered structure or behavior of the system. Look at the help icon to the left of each task for in-depth instructions in the IMG.

132) Which of the following statements are true regarding IMG Customizing?

   a. Documentation for IMG customizing is contained within IG itself
   b. IMG customizing can be performed by any user
   c. IMG customizing cab be performed only by users having specific roles
   d. Both a & c

Answer: d

Explanation:

IMG Customizing Documentation Documentation for IMG customizing is contained within the IMG itself. IMG customizing is performed by users assigned the following roles:

SAP_GRAC_SETUP for AC
SAP_GRC_SPC_CUSTOMIZING for PC
SAP_GRC_RM_CUSTOMIZING for RM

133) Business Users, such as Internal and External Auditors, are a subset of users that typically?

Note: There is more than one correct answer to the question

a. Reference non-transactional activities
b. Use the software to collect and analyze data to support business decisions
c. Serve as first support for end users
d. Fulfill a training role for other end users

Answer: a, b

Explanation:

Business Users are a subset of users that typically reference non-transactional activities. They use the software to collect and analyze data that help them support making business decisions. These users are focused on creating new strategies and making decisions based on information from a variety of sources.
Examples of business users include Internal and External Auditors, Risk Managers, and Compliance Managers.

134) Which of the following is not part of the project team?

a. Executives
b. Works Council
c. All end users
d. Power Users

Answer: c

Explanation:

Power Users are a subset of End Users who perform additional tasks beyond an End User's profile in a specific application area, for example, assigning user profiles. They often serve as first support and fulfill a training role for other end users.

Executives are responsible for business transformation and SAP selection and deployment. They have a very broad responsibility, but require expert assistance in specific areas, for example, they may be in charge of IT landscape strategy and the implementation of business requirements. They may also monitor the degree of user acceptance and system optimization after implementation.

A Works Council typically reviews generic user tasks against tasks that the Works Council represents. Popular in Europe, a Works Council has the task of promoting the interests both of the enterprise and of its workforce and serves to reduce workplace conflict by improving and systematizing communication channels. They give representatives of workers in large multinational companies a direct line of communication to top management and make sure that workers in different countries are all told the same thing at the same time about transnational policies and plans.

135) **A POC, prototype, or integration plan is typically developed during which phase?**

a. Implement
b. Configure
c. Optimize/Enhance
d. Design

Answer: d

Explanation:

Listed here are general tasks for the Design phase of implementation and may differ, depending on regions and business needs. For example, Security consultants typically ensure and discuss regional data security requirements and act as a NB Works Council liaison. When gathering parameters regarding processes, Security consultants may also define a responsibility matrix during this phase.

Access Control
- Analyze security and provisioning requirements
- Analyze and propose options for business process workflow solution
- Define a prototype or build a POC document
- Create a project plan and obtain approval
- Define or participate in evaluating architecture requirements

Process Control and Risk Management
- Collect and evaluate current compliance and risk requirements
- Evaluate gaps and analyze how to meet requirements with the GRC solution
- Develop POC and integration plan
- Design revised master data structures, roles and tasks
- Define IMG configuration requirements

Reporting

136) Which of the following reports are supported by SAP Business Objects GRC 10.0?

Note: There is more than one correct answer to the question

    a. Onscreen
    b. Excel
    c. Crystal Report
    d. Dashboards

Answer: a, b, c, d

Explanation:
SAP Business Objects GRC 10.0 allows the flexibility to deliver reports in different formats (Onscreen, Excel, Crystal Reports, and Dashboards) and with specific attributes. The flexibility provided by the Reporting Framework makes it easy to create variants that can be save and re-utilized at a later date or in continuing operations

137) Which of the following key capabilities are supported by GRC 10 harmonized Reporting Framework?

Note: There is more than one correct answer to the question

a. Configurable metadata
b. Harmonized presentation
c. Crystal Integration
d. Non SAP Integration

Answer: a, b, c

Explanation:

GRC10 harmonized reporting framework supports the following key capabilities:
- Harmonized presentation — Reports are presented in the information architecture based upon user authorization.
- Configurable metadata — Report structures and contents are configurable.
- Crystal integration — Reports can be displayed in Crystal while leveraging built-in ABAP List Viewer (ALV) functionality.

138) Which of the following reports might you find in the Master Data Work Center?

Note: There is more than one correct answer to the question

a. Reports related to compliance structure
b. Reports related to user authorization analysis
c. Reports related to audit analysis
d. Reports related to access rule detail

Answer: a, c

Explanation:

Reports related to compliance structure and audit analysis can be found in the Master Data work center. Reports related to user authorization analysis and access rules share a target user function and can be found in the Reports and Analytics work center under Access Management.

139) Which transaction is executed in order to maintain view cluster VC_GRFNREPCUST?

    a. SM35
    b. SM34
    c. SM36
    d. SM38

Answer: b

Explanation:

Reporting Framework for Customizing Reports To configure a new report without programming, you don't need to create the report from scratch. First, copy an existing report and then to make changes to it.

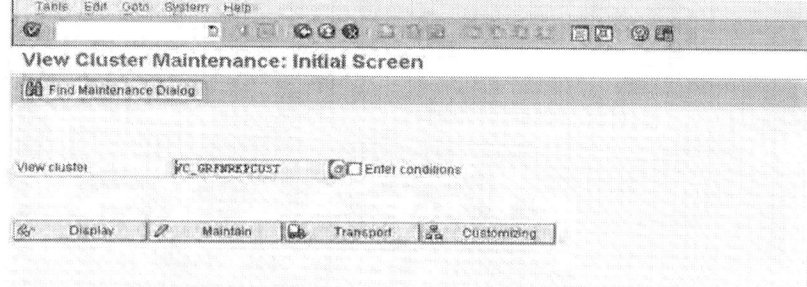

This transaction may be added to the IMG to make it easier to configure reports. As shown above, this is done by maintaining the view cluster VC_GRFNREPCUST.

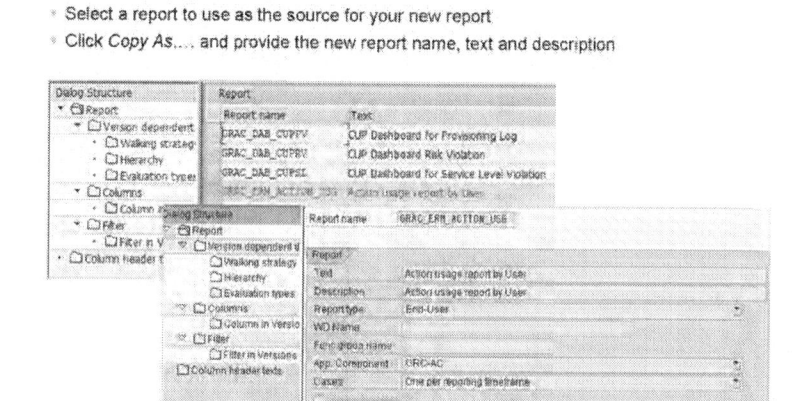

140) GRC 10 reports are delivered with three layout options of the following?

Note: There is more than one correct answer to the question

    a. ALV Grid Layout
    b. Crystal Layout Report
    c. General Crystal Layout
    d. Non crystal Layout

Answer: a, b, c

Explanation:

Crystal Integration GRC 10.0 reports are delivered with three layout options, which provide significant flexibility without programming.

GRC 10 reports are delivered with three layout options:

ALV Grid Layout:
- This solution generates reports in Web Dynpro ALV format.
- Users can reach the highest flexibility and analytical capability with the enablement of functionalities like: dynamic columns, foldable hierarchy nodes and navigation links.

ALV Grid Layout, Print via General Crystal Layout:
- This solution generates reports in Web Dynpro ALV format and allows users to export with a generic Crystal template.
- Users can have both the flexibility of dynamic columns as well as the report layout using a predefined Crystal Report template.

Crystal Report Layout:
- This solution generates reports in the Crystal Report layout.
- SAP provides out-of-box customizing Crystal Report templates for PC and RM. Graphics and charts are supported in this scenario.

Roles and Authorization

141) From which of the following area SAP roles are maintained to operate the Risk Management Application?

    a. SAP Net weaver back end
    b. Risk Management Application
    c. SAP Enterprise Portal
    d. Both a&b

Answer: a

Explanation:

SAP Net Weaver back-end - Technical SAP Roles are maintained to operate the Risk Management application. Transaction PFCG defines Risk Management specific roles such as Risk Manager or Risk

Owner. These roles contain the information about which actions and entities an end-user is allowed to perform once he/she is assigned the role. For example, Risk Owner (Business Role) can create and edit (actions) a risk (entity).

Risk Management application - Use the web front-end of the application to assign end-users to Business User roles and to entities such as risks, opportunities, and organizations. In the example above, Mr. Miller is assigned to be Risk Manager for Organization Unit ABC.

SAP Enterprise Portal - The portal role assigned to the end-user determines how and where the Risk Management specific information, such as the order and number of visible work center, is presented.

142) Which of the following role definition is required to operate the Risk Management?

   a. FN_BASE
   b. FN_ALL
   c. FN_DISPLAY
   d. FN_BUSINESS_USERS

Answer: a

Explanation:

A system administrator can use transaction PFCG in SAP User and Role Management to modify these role definitions:

- **FN_BASE:** is the basic (minimal) technical role required to operate the Risk Management application. This role contains all necessary authorizations to make the necessary customizing settings in IMG for the Risk Management application.
   This role does not contain any authorizations for the portal interface.
- **FN_ALL:** contains authorization for administrative functions in IMG customizing, as well as power user authorization in the application. When this role is assigned to a user, the user becomes a power user.
- **FN_DISPLAY:** enables an end-user with this role to display all risk management information. This role is useful for external auditors who wish to check the system settings and view content, but should not be able to make changes to the application.
- **FN_BUSINESS_USER:** authorizes the user to perform actions on only assigned entities in risk management.

143) Which of the following is the default portal role for the Risk Management application is shipped as SAP Enterprise Portal Content?

   a. Com.sap.grc
   b. Com.sap.grc_all

c. Com.sap.grc_rm_all
   d. Com.sap.grc.rm.Role_all

Answer: d

Explanation:

Portal Role

• The Portal Role maintained in SAP Enterprise Portal defines where and how the Risk Management content is presented to the end-user
• Each end-user needs to have a Portal Role assigned to access the Risk Management application

A default portal role, com.sap.grc.rm.Role_All, for the Risk Management application is shipped as SAP Enterprise Portal Content.

The role can be copied and/or adjusted to match the target portal and information structure, for example, remove or rename tabs from the default role.

144) Which of the following concept is primarily targeted for temporary redistribution and reassignment of work?

   a. Portal Role
   b. Delegation
   c. Replacement
   d. Reassignment

Answer: b

Explanation:

Delegation

• Delegation allows a user to act as delegate in the Risk Management application for a second user
• The delegate works on behalf of the second user, including all authorizations and workflow assignments

- Delegation can be given for own authorization or defined centrally depending on the Special Authorization assigned to the Business User role

In the default SAP Enterprise Portal role the entries for Central Own Delegation can be found in the "User Access" Work Center.

The delegation concept is primarily targeted for temporary redistribution and reassignment of work, for example, during vacation or maternity leave of an employee. It also supports a permanent delegation of authorizations that might be applicable for some roles, for example, Executive Assistant acting on behalf of the CEO/CFO in the risk management application.

These applications allow the definition of delegates through a step-by-step procedure. The delegate can change his current authorization he is working with by using "Change Delegation" on the upper right side of the Risk Management start pages. "Own Delegation" allows the definition of own delegates whereas "Central Delegation"

Key Risk Indicators

145) A key Risk indicator can be following?

    a. Estimating the risk event
    b. Quantitative
    c. Qualitative
    d. All of the above

Answer: d

Explanation:

Key Risk Indicators A Key Risk Indicator (KRI) is a forward-looking measure that provides a basis for estimating the likelihood of a risk event. A KRI can be quantitative (e.g. turnover rate in a business unit), qualitative (e.g. adequacy of a system). To be useful, a KRI always has to be linked to one of the risk drivers (or cause).

Historical performance trend is used as the basis for a forward-looking perspective. KRIs provide early warning signals by highlighting trends and changes in risk level by monitoring changes in actual performance.

146) **Which of the following are the examples of KRI that can use data from SAP and Non SAP Systems?**

Note: There is more than one correct answer to the question

a. Cash position
b. Service provision
c. Warranty claims
d. Employee Utilization

Answer: a, b, c, d

Explanation:

KRIs can use data from SAP and non-SAP systems. Examples are:

- Cash position by day/currency (SAP ERP Financials)
- Quality of Service Provision (SAP Supply Chain Management)
- Number of warranty claims (SAP ERP Operations)
- Number of credit breaches per month (ROME Credit Risk)
- Employee Utilization (SAP Human Capital Management)
- Illness Rate (SAP Human Capital Management)

The following should be taken into consideration when designing KRIs:

- Design the best KRIs independent of data availability; use interim KRIs if desired data not available
- Work with the business to design the KRIs.
- Keep KRIs simple to be understood.
- Establish KRIs that can be used across all business areas and locations if possible.
- Make sure KRIs are quantifiable.
- Use pre-defined escalation criteria for management actions (e.g. Acceptable; Acceptable but Watch; Unacceptable)

147) Following needs to be addressed when evaluating the potential KRI's?

   Note: There is more than one correct answer to the question

   a. Can KRI trigger levels established
   b. Is KRI loading enough
   c. Does Historical data Exists
   d. Is KRI data accurate and reliable

Answer: a, b, c, d

Explanation:

KRI Design Steps Certain design steps should be undertaken before implementing a Key Risk Indicator in SAP Business Objects Risk Management. To start, you need a specific risk event for which the KRIs will be used. A KRI is not a stand-alone metrics; it is a measure that provides a basis for estimating the likelihood of a specific risk event.

Start by asking the following questions when evaluating potential KRIs:

- Can the KRI be measured at a frequency that is low enough to identify a potential risk event?
- Can KRI trigger levels be established?
- Can clear escalation criteria be established?
- Is the KRI leading enough?
- Is there a clear owner for the KRI data?
- Is the KRI data available in a SAP or non-SAP system?
- Does historical data exist?
- Is the KRI data accurate and reliable?

Next, the potential KRIs should be rated in terms of their relationship to the risk event drivers. That is, KRIs deemed to have a "strong" relationship to a driver should be implemented over a KRI that has a "weak" relationship to the same driver. Once you have selected the "strongest" KRIs, you are ready to start implementing them in SAP Business Objects Risk Management. This begins with the design of the SAP Query.

148) Which of the following is required if the KRI data resides in a non-SAP System?

   a. SAP query
   b. RFC creation
   c. Web service connector
   d. Both a & c

Answer: c

Explanation:

SAP Query SAP Query is a tool used to extract KRI data in SAP system. Once you know what data you need and from which SAP system (based on the KRI design), you should seek the help of a SAP Query resource.

Similarly, if the KRI data resides in a non-SAP system, you will need a resource to design and develop the Web Service connector from the source system to SAP Business Objects Risk Management.

149) Which of the following are the prerequisites must be fulfilled before you implement a KRI?

  a. IMG customizing activates to be completed
  b. KRI template to be created
  c. KRI template to be activated
  d. Both a & b

Answer: a, b

Explanation:

KRI Implementation The following prerequisites must be fulfilled before you can implement a KRI:

- Complete the IMG customizing activities on system connectivity for Key Risk Indicators.
- Create the KRI template that will be referenced when implementing the KRI

150) Which of the following are the KRI implementation status definitions?

Note: There is more than one correct answer to the question

  a. Draft
  b. Active
  c. Scheduled
  d. Cancelled

Answer: a, b, d

Explanation:

The KRI implementation status definitions are follows:

• *Draft:* The KRI has not yet been sent for implementations. Draft KRIs will be invisible in the Linkage Corridor and in the Usage Corridor. They will only be visible in the Implementation Corridor, and can only be deleted or asked for implementation.

• *Active:* The KRI implementation is being used.

• *Cancelled:* A cancelled KRI implementation cannot be reactivated. All related instantiations are switched to "cancelled" in their own statuses once the implementations are cancelled.

Printed in Great Britain
by Amazon.co.uk, Ltd.,
Marston Gate.